"If the quest for certainty has become a habit that you just can't break, thi[s] friend. You'll get a set of easy-to-learn skills that will teach you to trust those pesky doubts that come with them. This is just what you need to take back your life."

—**Reid Wilson, PhD**, author of *Stopping the Noise in Your Head*

"Reassurance seeking compulsions can be exhausting for obsessive-compulsive disorder (OCD) sufferers and their loved ones. This practical book does a thorough job of providing you with evidence-based tools based in cognitive behavioral therapy (CBT) that will help you eliminate reassurance compulsions so that you can gain trust in yourself and live your life more freely."

—**Kim Rockwell-Evans, PhD**, founder of OCD and Anxiety Specialists of Dallas, and author of *Breaking the Rules of OCD*

"Amanda Petrik-Gardner has taken her sound clinical skills and created an easily digestible OCD workbook! This book is gold for anyone who is looking to jump-start their recovery. Therapists will also find this workbook to be a valuable supplement to any therapy session."

—**Natasha Daniels**, OCD therapist, and author of *Crushing OCD Workbook for Kids*

"Amanda Petrik-Gardner's excellent workbook presents a number of techniques and strategies for reducing the reassurance seeking that maintains OCD. She also includes one of the first-ever set of self-help instructions for applying the power of inference-based CBT to overcoming OCD."

—**Carl Robbins, LCPC**, senior clinician and director of training at The Anxiety and Stress Disorders Institute of Maryland

"This workbook is truly transformative for anyone passionate about the OCD treatment and recovery journey. Providing a *groundbreaking* shift in perspective, it enhanced my understanding personally and professionally. It explores overlooked forms of compulsive reassurance seeking and offers accessible, evidence-based steps for reclaiming life. A must-read for clinicians, individuals with OCD, family members, and faith leaders—it compassionately reshapes approaches to addressing reassurance seeking within the context of OCD."

—**Rev. Katie O'Dunne**, faith/OCD specialist, and founder of the Stick with the Ick Virtual Community

"*The Compulsive Reassurance Seeking Workbook* is a beacon of hope for individuals facing the challenges of reassurance seeking. Amanda, an expert in the field, has created a comprehensive guide that skillfully addresses the complexities of reassurance seeking while transforming the difficulties of this disorder into a manageable and empowering process. A must-read for anyone seeking practical solutions and lasting changes."

>   —**Jenna Overbaugh, LPC**, creator of The OCD and Anxiety Recovery Blueprint,
>   and host of the *All The Hard Things* podcast

"Petrik-Gardner writes with warmth and clarity about a symptom common to all subtypes of OCD. She provides tools and frameworks for readers to develop awareness of common reassurance compulsions, challenge their validity, and ultimately break the OCD cycle. She also deftly explores the impact of reassurance seeking on relationships, and how to harness truly effective support in your recovery."

>   —**Amy Mariaskin, PhD**, licensed psychologist, director of the Nashville OCD & Anxiety
>   Treatment Center, and author of *Thriving in Relationships When You Have OCD*

The

Compulsive Reassurance Seeking Workbook

CBT Skills to Help You
Live with Confidence and
Break the Cycle of
Obsessive-Compulsive Disorder

AMANDA PETRIK-GARDNER, LCPC

New Harbinger Publications, Inc.

Publisher's Note

NEW HARBINGER PUBLICATIONS is a registered trademark of New Harbinger Publications, Inc.

New Harbinger Publications is an employee-owned company.

Cover design by Amy Daniel

Acquired by Jess O'Brien

Edited by Joyce Wu

Printed in the United States of America

26   25   24

10   9   8   7   6   5   4   3   2   1   First Printing

Contents

Foreword

Will I be judged by the way I write this foreword? In fact, am I even doing this correctly? What if I completely missed the mark? I should probably hand this off to someone else to avoid looking incompetent. My brain says: *Run, Hide,* and *Avoid.* It screams, *This is too risky for you and your career. What are you doing?* But, here is what we know—no matter how many times I ask someone to read this foreword to give me their opinion, those nasty feelings of doubt, uncertainty, danger, and anxiety would still linger.

That is the trap with reassurance seeking. It's hardly ever good enough.

So here I am, writing a foreword anyway. Do you know why? Because that's how we improve, grow, and learn. I choose to accept the perceived risk of messing up this foreword and am open to all possible outcomes.

That is exactly what Amanda Petrik-Gardner expounds on in this *Compulsive Reassurance Seeking Workbook.* It teaches many basic principles that most miss because they simply don't have the right tools. Illustrated simply, you're going to learn how to recognize your compulsions, how they can be damaging to use, and here's the best part...how to stop them and retrain your brain.

Reassurance seeking can provide temporary relief from anxiety, and because of this the body says, "Good job! You kept yourself safe." The brain then creates a special note tucked away deep inside that says, "Okay, next time you're anxious, you know what to do...I mean, it worked last time." Thus, keeping someone stuck in the never-ending cycle of this reassurance seeking just to find that short-lived relief.

Hey, I don't blame you. If it works, it works. But what we're wanting is long-term relief. That is what you're getting with this workbook. Its emphasis is on reassurance seeking, a common compulsion often associated with OCD. This workbook helps you really know and understand yourself, how you might get stuck in the OCD cycle, and what compulsions you continue to do (even ones you may not know you are doing) that ultimately keep you trapped.

Oh, and Amanda doesn't just talk about reassurance. She gives you straightforward guidance on what to do about it. To make meaningful changes in your life. To teach your brain something new and create an action plan to do so. Sure, it's fun to learn, but it's better to do and experience. As I've always said, we can talk about OCD and stay in the same spot, or we can be doers and actually grow, learn, and recover.

Imagine you've started a new job and all you did was watch the training videos over and over again for days on end. How will you progress without applying what you've learned? In fact, you'd probably have those videos memorized, a really cool skill. But that won't take you very far. That is where the exercises and prompts provided in this workbook come in. It turns you from a learner to an action-taker.

Reassurance seeking in many forms is one of the biggest compulsions we do. It's important not only to disrupt the patterns but continually teach the brain that we can handle the uncertainty and distress that comes along with life. You ultimately learn that if you're not reacting to the urges that prompt you to ask for reassurance, maybe your brain needs to stop sending them your way. This is where the magic happens—learning to trust in yourself again and actually having a game plan to take you where you want to be.

Now, I do feel a little strange providing reassurance that you made a good choice by purchasing Amanda's workbook. But what's great is that you don't need me to tell you because you'll experience it yourself through your own learning and efforts. In short, that is exactly where this workbook takes you. Learn through lived experience and not through what someone tells you (which means you'll have to put some work into it, but it's so worth it).

I am confident in your ability to learn new things, change your behaviors, and break free of compulsive reassurance seeking. You've trusted in yourself enough to make it this far—think of how much further you can go. With the confidence you gain without needing reassurance, you'll learn that trust actually means you may have chosen to relinquish the words *why* and *what if*. Your job now isn't to always know—your job is to live, and that is exactly what Amanda provides you throughout this workbook. Stay confident. Build new habits and find joy in everything you do. You can do it!

Best wishes,

Nathan Peterson, LCSW
OCD and Anxiety Counseling
OCD and Anxiety on YouTube

PART 1

What Are OCD and Reassurance Seeking Compulsions?

CHAPTER 1

OCD

Jannette feels anxious when she drives to work. She avoids driving as much as possible by asking her husband to run errands, shopping online, or walking if her destination is within a mile. However, she does not want to lose her job, so she continues to drive to work. What does Jannette fear? Every day, she worries she may have hit a pedestrian and did not notice. She experiences extreme anxiety anytime she hits a bump or a pothole, but also when the road is smooth because "maybe [she] hit someone and did not feel it." Jannette states that she fears she could do something so awful, even by accident, that she gets punished by the law or a higher being. Due to all this anxiety, Jannette checks. She checks a lot. She checks her car daily, from headlight to taillight, to see if there are any scratches or dents. She checks the streets for dead bodies. She checks her memory, to see if she can recall any details she may not have noticed the first time. She also seeks help from loved ones, asking her husband daily if he believes she hit someone (even though he was not even present during the drive!). She texts her mom, her biggest support, to inquire if she would be okay if it was later found out that she hit someone.

Jannette's story is a typical example of the clients I work with every day in my private practice. Can you relate to any aspects of her experience? You may or may not have the same content and fears she has, but I bet the nagging doubt, intense anxiety, and urge to "make it go away" all feel similar. Jannette is struggling with a mental health diagnosis called obsessive-compulsive disorder (OCD). Her fear is that she hit a pedestrian, so then she engages in many reassurance compulsions to relieve this doubt. Before we explore reassurance compulsions more in depth, and how to decrease them, let's consider the basics of what OCD is and how it works. We'll break down OCD into two parts: obsessions and compulsions.

Obsessions and Compulsions

Obsessions can come in the form of thoughts, images, urges, commands, or sensations. They are persistent, meaning they are nonstop, constant, and determined to stick around. Obsessions are anxiety provoking for one or several of these reasons:

- There is a feared consequence if they were to come true.

- They simply feel uncomfortable.

- They latch onto a vulnerable topic for you, such as a value of yours.

And most importantly, obsessions are unwanted and ego-dystonic, meaning the obsessions go against or are inconsistent with your character, self-concept, and values. Obsessions may sound like:

- *What if the toilet is contaminated and I get sick after sitting on it?*

- *Maybe I will never know my sexual orientation for sure!*

- *What if I just stabbed my spouse in the middle of the night?*

- *What if I offended God?*

- *I need everything lined up perfectly otherwise it will feel uncomfortable.*

- *What if I'm attracted to my brother?!*

- *Is my partner "the one"?*

- *What if that pain in my stomach is actually cancer?*

- *What if I could still get in trouble for that situation that happened to me twenty years ago?*

EXERCISE: Take a moment to identify a few of your obsessions. If you are having difficulty identifying these, ask yourself if there are any sticky thoughts (but also images, urges, commands, or sensations) that you cannot get out of your head. These sticky thoughts produce anxiety and continue to nag at you, no matter how hard you try not to let them. They might come in the form of "What if..." or "Maybe..." Jot those down here:

_____

_____

_____

_____

_____

Great work! Now we will move on to compulsions. Compulsions are repetitive rituals aimed at 1) making the anxiety go away, 2) making the obsession go away, or 3) preventing a feared consequence. These rituals can be mental or behavioral. Behavioral compulsions are overt, meaning they are observable by others. These may include:

- Washing your hands
- Physically checking door locks
- Confessing to your priest
- Arranging the items on your bookshelf
- Walking in and out of a doorway repeatedly
- Asking reassurance questions
- Apologizing to loved ones
- Behavioral avoidance (not doing something)
- Tapping the countertop five times
- Stepping over cracks on the sidewalk
- Googling for answers

EXERCISE: Identify any behavioral compulsions you engage in. If you are having difficulty identifying these, ask yourself, *What do I do, repetitively, in order to make the anxiety or the obsession go away or to make sure nothing bad happens?* You can also peek back at the obsessions you listed above and ask yourself, *What did I do to make myself feel better after having that thought?* Jot these down here:

_____

_____

_____

_____

_____

_____

Mental compulsions can be more difficult to recognize, as they are unseen. Others will not notice you are doing this mental process, and you may not even notice it either, as sometimes it can feel automatic as opposed to a deliberate choice. However, mental compulsions are still a choice, albeit sometimes a more difficult choice to resist. To make mental compulsions even trickier—you may confuse them with obsessions as they are both occurring mentally. If you find yourself confused by whether something is an obsession or a mental compulsion, here is your reminder: Obsessions are unwanted and cause anxiety. Compulsions are tasks you choose to engage in to relieve anxiety. Here are several examples of mental compulsions:

- Self-reassurance
- Counting in your head
- Praying in your head
- Mental reviewing
- Cognitive avoidance (trying not to think something)
- Challenging your thoughts
- Thinking of your happy place
- Imagining a "stop" sign when your obsession comes up
- Repeating lucky words or phrases in your head
- Problem-solving
- Rumination

EXERCISE: Identify any mental compulsions you engage in. If you are having difficulty identifying these, ask yourself, *Is there anything I am doing in my head to make my anxiety go away?* or *Am I doing anything in my head to make the obsession go away?* Jot these down here:

_____

_____

_____

_____

_____

_____

Now, anything could become a compulsion. Even everyday tasks like brushing your teeth, watching television, driving to work, or lying down in bed. To illustrate whether an action is a compulsion, let's look at washing our hands because they are dirty, or praying as part of our faith—neither behavior is inherently bad. In fact, many people engage in those same two behaviors in healthy ways. But whether the behavior crosses over to a compulsion depends on the reason, or function, behind the behavior. The function of compulsions is, once again, 1) to make the anxiety go away, 2) to make the obsession go away, or 3) to prevent a feared consequence (as opposed to engaging in a behavior because it is a value, because you enjoy it, or because it serves a purpose).

EXERCISE: Let me share two different scenarios with the *same* behavior. Can you tell which is a compulsion and which is a value? Circle the example you believe is a compulsion.

1. Marcus is cooking dinner. He just finished holding the raw chicken and throwing it into a skillet. He goes to wash his hands so that he does not contaminate the remaining food he has to cook.

2. Marcus finished cooking dinner; however, he continues to feel distressed. He continues to think about the raw chicken he touched even though he already washed his hands. He thinks, *What if my hands are still contaminated?* So, he stands at the sink, washing his hands for twenty minutes.

In scenario 1, Marcus is washing his hands out of a value. He washes his hands after touching raw meat. This is not a repetitive behavior that he feels the urge to do over and over again. He is not feeling anxious, nor is he thinking that washing his hands will make anxiety go away. While washing his hands does prevent a consequence (something becoming contaminated), he wants to do the behavior because there is an actual health benefit that aligns with his beliefs and value system.

In scenario 2, Marcus is washing his hands excessively, as most individuals would agree that twenty minutes is unnecessary. Plus, he had already washed them before! He does not want to wash them again; however, he feels like he has to, to stop the anxiety, stop the thoughts, and make sure he does not contaminate anything. In scenario 2, Marcus's hand washing is a compulsion. I bet you circled the second scenario!

EXERCISE: Here is another set of scenarios with the *same* behavior. Can you tell which is a compulsion and which is a value? Circle the example you believe is a compulsion.

1. Rebecca is at church. She hasn't smiled once during the service and wonders if she is a bad person and if not having smiled is a sin. *What if I will be punished for this?* Rebecca immediately starts praying. She feels momentary relief; however, when she returns home, she has the same

thought. *What if I'm going to be punished for that?* She prays again before bed and finds herself praying throughout the week to feel better.

2. Rebecca is at church. She says a prayer for her neighbor who recently lost his job.

Which example did you circle? Probably the first, as Rebecca is repetitively praying to relieve the anxiety of her obsession, *What if I sinned because I did not smile in the service?* While Rebecca does value her faith, in scenario 1 her praying was not driven by her values. The praying was an attempt to seek relief and reassurance that she is not a bad person. In the second scenario, Rebecca enjoys praying for those she cares about in a genuine manner. If she does choose to do it repetitively, such as every night before bed, it is done out of a place of peace and her values.

EXERCISE: Do you have a compulsion that could also double as a value, depending on the function? Make note of it here, as well as how you will be able to distinguish between compulsion and value. This will assist you in the future in case you get stuck wondering, *Is this part of my OCD or am I wanting to do this?*

_____

_____

_____

Diagnosis

Now that you have a good understanding of obsessions and compulsions, let's consider the formal criteria for OCD. The American Psychiatric Association (2022) explains that OCD consists of obsessions, compulsions, or both being present.

You may have heard the term "Pure O," which implies that you have OCD with purely obsessions and no compulsions. But what this term actually reflects is that the compulsions tend to be "invisible," as Pure O typically involves mental compulsions. Despite being unseen, compulsions are still present even for this subtype.

The APA's diagnostic criteria for OCD also include the time-consuming nature of the disorder. These obsessions do not occupy your mind for a mere couple minutes out of your day or week. Rather, these obsessions become stuck and persistent for hours. According to the Yale-Brown Obsessive-Compulsive Scale (Goodman et al. 1989), the standard OCD assessment, less than an hour per day of having obsessive thoughts is typically considered mild. Moderate severity includes one to three hours per day, while severe severity would be three to eight hours per day, and extreme severity would be over eight hours per day.

The same severity scales are utilized for compulsions. These repetitive rituals are not a simple few seconds out of your day. How much time per day do you spend on obsessions and how much time do you spend on compulsions?

_____

_____

_____

Due to the time-consuming nature of OCD and the high level of distress that comes with it, there is often an impairment in functioning as well. What this actually looks like, though, varies from person to person. Your OCD may be causing conflict with your significant other or family. OCD might be making it difficult to study and pass your classes or to obtain a job. OCD could also be so time consuming that it is keeping you from completing the things you want to do around the house. How has OCD impacted your functioning?

_____

_____

_____

The last criterion of OCD verifies that these symptoms are not better accounted for by another physical or mental health disorder or due to a substance. There are a variety of mental health disorders, including anxiety disorders, eating disorders, or obsessive-compulsive and related disorders that may better explain your symptoms. These possibly include, but are not limited to:

- Generalized anxiety disorder—persistent and excessive worry about a variety of topics like work, school, finances, relationships, health, and more

- Anorexia nervosa—eating disorder characterized by a fear of being overweight and a distorted body image

- Trichotillomania—hair pulling disorder

- Excoriation—skin picking disorder

- Body dysmorphic disorder—preoccupation with physical appearance and a perceived physical flaw

- Hoarding—difficulty getting rid of possessions that are no longer needed

As you read through the criteria of OCD, you could be experiencing a lot of feelings. There may be relief, as you finally realize that the symptoms you have been experiencing have a name and a treatment. You may be experiencing fear, as you wonder if you should seek a professional diagnosis and what the future will look like for you. You may be experiencing anger, as you have spent years and years getting misdiagnosed and mistreated.

All of these feelings are valid, and you are worthy of the proper diagnosis and treatment. If you have yet to be properly diagnosed by an OCD specialist, now is the time to reach out. One valuable resource to find a specialist and begin that process is the International OCD Foundation. Getting treatment could be the beginning of a new life for you—less anxiety, improved relationships, a better ability to be present in the moment, doing the things you value doing.

If you have some hesitation to move forward, though, that is understandable and quite common. It can feel scary to call a psychiatrist or a therapist. It can be even scarier to share your obsessions and compulsions with someone and not know what their reaction will be. Please know that OCD specialists have heard and seen it all, and maybe even experienced something similar. You deserve to feel better.

OCD Myths

It can be helpful to discuss what OCD isn't, in order to better understand what it is. Here are the biggest myths about OCD that are often seen among the general public, on television and in movies, and on social media. Have you heard any of these myths? Have you ever thought of them yourself? Provide yourself compassion; much of the general public believes these same myths.

OCD is a love of cleaning and organizing! OCD isn't a love of anything, and that includes cleaning and organizing. While contamination OCD and just-right OCD are common OCD subtypes and may involve cleaning and organizing compulsions, these subtypes are distressing and not enjoyable. You may excessively clean as a compulsion and look very tidy; however, you are not doing this because you want to. You are doing this because of an awful feeling saying you must do it—otherwise, you are doomed.

OCD is funny or beneficial. You may have seen "I'm so OCD" memes on social media that portray OCD, anxiety, and intrusive thoughts as humorous, quirky, or beneficial. While memes like these do a little to normalize talking about mental health, they in fact cause more harm than good by trivializing and mischaracterizing OCD. OCD is a serious condition that goes beyond liking order, cleanliness, or punctuality. It can be debilitating to people who have it and deserves to be discussed with respect. No one would ever choose to have OCD, and there are no perks.

People love their compulsions. If you ask any person diagnosed with OCD if they love their compulsions, you would get a resounding no. Excessive hand washing can cause chapped and bleeding hands. Excessive googling takes up too much time and keeps people from living their lives how they genuinely want to. Excessive lock checking leads to significant time wasted and frustration because you just don't know how to stop. No one loves these experiences.

If you think it, you will be it! There is an affirmation that has gone around for years: If you think it, you will be it! Or similarly, "You are what you think." This affirmation may be motivational for the general public, but for people with OCD, it can cause intense anxiety. You may become more fearful hearing "You are what you think" when you have sexual obsessions that make you wonder if you are attracted to your sibling. Thoughts are simply thoughts and do not have a magical power to make you become anything.

Certain themes, like harm and sexual obsessions, are dangerous. I could write a whole chapter on the horror stories I have heard, where OCD was assessed incorrectly and the provider felt their client posed a threat to themselves or someone else. There is a significant difference between harm obsessions and being homicidal. There is a significant difference between suicidal obsessions and suicidal ideation. And there is a significant difference between sexual obsessions and engaging in sexual acts like rape, incest, or pedophilia. Obsessions are unwanted and distressing for a reason: they go against your character, values, and who you genuinely are as a person. Having an obsession does not mean you will act on it. You are the least likely person to act on your obsessions, because they are so terrifying to you.

Just stop thinking that! **Just don't do the compulsions.** I wish it were that easy! In fact, the more you try to stop thinking about something, the more it comes up. Have you heard the cliché "Don't think about the white elephant in the room"? Trying not to think of something will only make it pop up more. Thought suppression is a mental compulsion and it simply does not work. While it would be nice to simply halt all compulsions immediately, most people find that a little difficult to do. They need support; they need a plan; they need strategies; they need baby steps.

The OCD Cycle and Obsessional Sequence

Now that you have a good understanding of what OCD is, there are a couple different ways to visualize how the cycle works. I will put these concepts into easy-to-follow visuals so you may practice them both. You may even connect with one model better than another and that is okay! There is no right choice.

Your OCD Cycle

Exposure and response prevention, which will be discussed in more detail in chapter 7, states that obsessions are random, intrusive thoughts. They are then misappraised, or misjudged, as having a lot more meaning and power than they truly do. Due to this misappraisal, anxiety ensues (Steketee 1999). The thought now seems scary, even though it is simply a thought! Because there is now anxiety present, and most people do not want to feel anxious, you try to make it go away. Well, in OCD, trying to make a thought go away is a compulsion. Those compulsions may provide short-term relief but in the long run only fuel the cycle. Here is a visual of the OCD cycle, using Marcus—who was concerned about contamination from touching chicken even after he washed his hands—as an example:

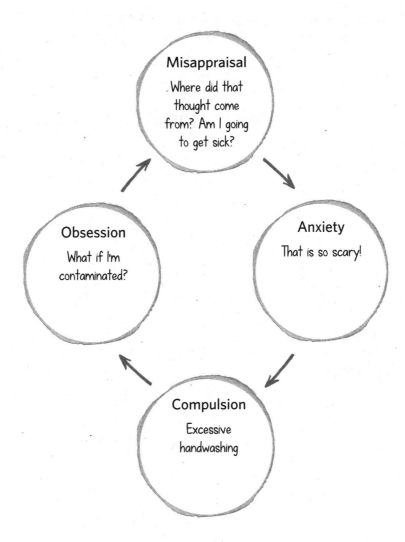

EXERCISE: Try filling out an OCD cycle! Pick one of the obsessions you identified in the earlier exercise. Enter that fear in the "obsession" circle in the blank OCD cycle on the following page.

Then, explore your reaction to having that thought. Maybe your reaction was *Why did I have that thought? What's wrong with me?* Or maybe your reaction was a feared consequence of that thought. Enter this reaction, or how you appraised that thought, under "misappraisal."

Next, brainstorm what it is about that obsession and misappraisal that causes anxiety. If it didn't cause anxiety, then it would never have become an obsession. Maybe it just feels awful. Maybe you worry you can't live with that obsession. Maybe the feared consequence is so awful, it fills your body with dread. Enter this in the "anxiety" circle.

Last, what compulsion might you feel the urge to do in response to this anxiety? There may even be more than one. Be sure to think about mental compulsions as well. List these in the "compulsion" circle.

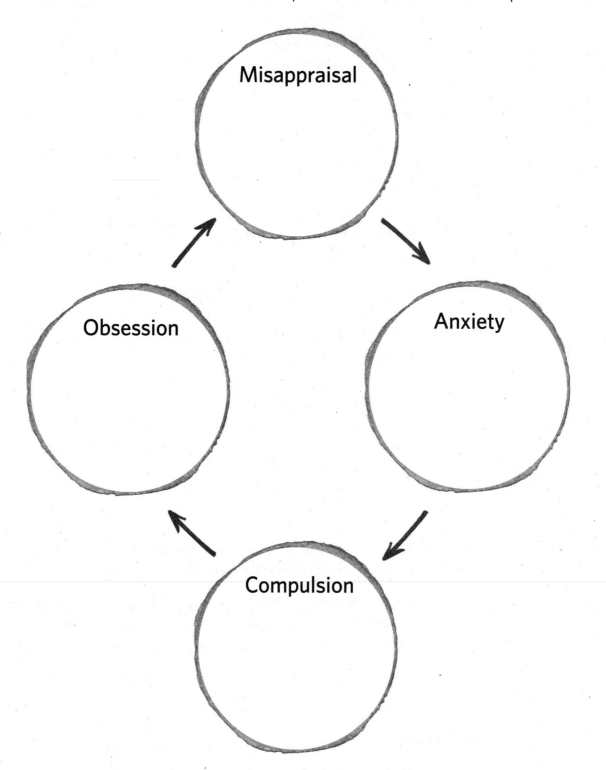

Congratulations! You have completed your OCD cycle. If you would like to practice this again with a different obsession, you can download the worksheet at http://www.newharbinger.com/52502.

Obsessional Sequence

Inference-based cognitive behavioral therapy (I-CBT), to be discussed further in chapter 9, suggests that random thoughts are not so random. They are actually inferences, meaning conclusions you come to through evidence and reasoning. An inference comes in the form of a doubt, which I-CBT defines as "a questioning of information, knowledge, assumptions or hunches one already possesses" (O'Connor and Aardema 2012). With OCD though, our doubts are obsessional doubts, meaning there is no direct evidence in the here and now to make them credible. In fact, someone experiencing obsessional doubts may distrust information in the here and now, instead overly relying on possibility and information built in the imagination. Before you know it, you're in the middle of an obsessional sequence, illustrated by figure 3.

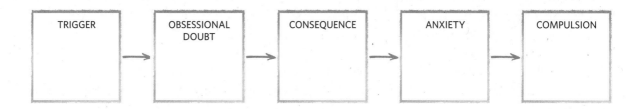

The first step to the obsessional sequence is a trigger. This may be an external trigger, like holding a kitchen knife, or an internal trigger, like thinking about a time when you were cooking and chopping vegetables with a kitchen knife.

The trigger leads to an obsessional doubt, step 2 of the obsessional sequence, which often sounds like "What if…" or "Maybe…" Obsessional doubts may sound like:

- *What if I am a serial killer?*

- *Maybe I could get sick from touching the doorknob.*

- *What if the bump in the road was actually a pedestrian?*

- *Maybe my partner isn't "the one."*

Next, there is a consequence to that doubt. If there weren't a consequence, you probably wouldn't get stuck on the obsession to begin with! The consequence causes anxiety in some manner, which leads to the last step of the sequence—engaging in compulsions to relieve that anxiety.

Let's use the example about Rebecca from earlier to demonstrate the obsessional sequence. As a reminder, while Rebecca was at church, she became fearful she sinned because she was not smiling during the service. This led to excessive prayer, even once she returned home.

TRIGGER	OBSESSIONAL DOUBT	CONSEQUENCE	ANXIETY	COMPULSION
Noticing I was not smiling during the church service.	What if I sinned?	I will be punished.	That's my biggest fear, I can't handle that!	Excessive praying

EXERCISE: Your turn to fill in the obsessional sequence. Pick one of the obsessions you identified in the earlier exercise. You may even use the same obsession you practiced in the OCD cycle exercise, or you may pick a brand new one. Enter that in the "obsessional doubt" box.

Now, identify what triggered you before that obsessional doubt came up. Maybe it was a situation, a person, an object, or a place. Or it might have been something you thought; a memory, an image, a random thought. Put this trigger in the "trigger" box.

Next, what is the consequence of your doubt? Describe what would happen if your doubt came true. Place that in your "consequence" box.

What about that consequence makes you so anxious? What would that mean for you if that consequence happened? Enter this in the "anxiety" box.

Last, what compulsion did you feel the urge to do because of this anxiety? Enter that in your final "compulsion" box. To do this exercise again, visit http://www.newharbinger.com/52502 to download a free copy of the obsessional sequence.

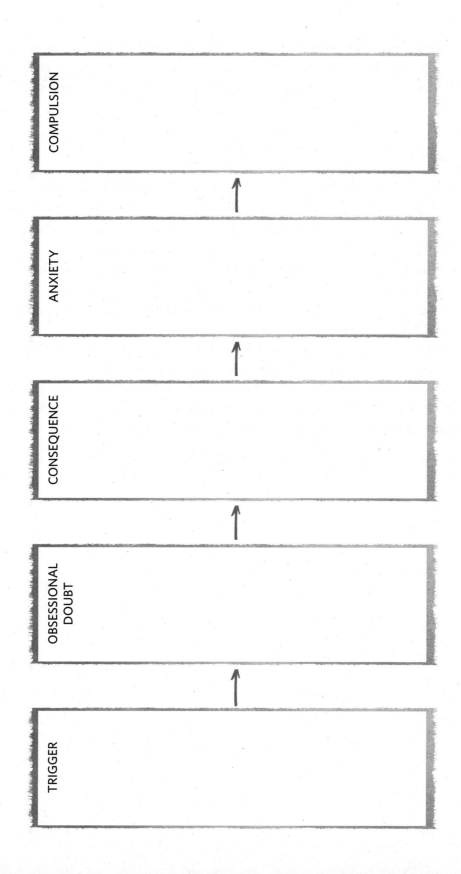

Let me share my experience with contamination obsessions and how OCD presented itself. See if you can identify different components of my OCD, such as the obsession, compulsion, a consequence, and maybe even a trigger. I will then share examples of what my OCD cycle and obsessional sequence could look like.

My Story

For as long as I can remember, I was overly concerned with germs and contamination surrounding trash cans. But not from touching the trash or the inside of a trash can (even though I greatly dislike that too). I was also concerned about anything around and above the trash can. The wall behind the trash can. The ground below it. Even the air above it. It wasn't until adulthood that I realized this was unusual, as I observed others freely and casually exist around a trash can without panicking. I witnessed people scrape food off their plates into a trash can, and then continue to eat off of that same plate. I thought this was insane and dangerous even though it never came in contact with the trash can! The plate is now contaminated! You can't eat off that same plate now!

Due to this fear of contamination, I avoided doing things like peeling a cucumber above the trash can. I can recall one specific incident when I wanted to peel a cucumber above the trash can but avoided it. I felt certain that the cucumber would be contaminated by airborne germs above it or that I would be dirty. The cucumber would be inedible then, so from that point on, I peeled the cucumber on the counter and then threw the peels away.

My OCD cycle may have looked something like this:

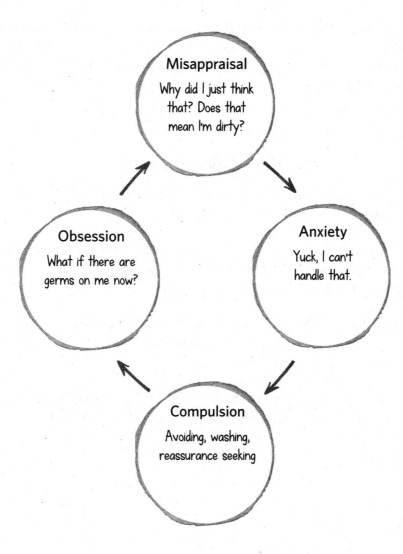

The obsession could also be "What if my cucumber is contaminated now?" with the misappraisal that the cucumber is inedible.

My obsessional sequence might look like:

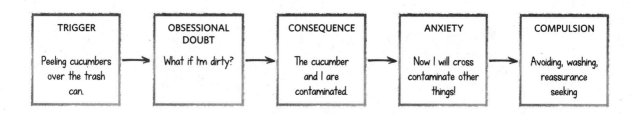

You will notice that both the OCD cycle and the obsessional sequence end in compulsions, pulling us further into our obsessional doubt and worsening our OCD. The OCD cycle and obsessional sequence are self-reinforcing, which is why it is so important that you address the compulsions, including the very common reassurance compulsions! Continue reading and learn more about reassurance compulsions in chapter 2!

Key Takeaways

✓ Obsessions are thoughts, images, urges, sensations, or commands that feel like they are "stuck." They are persistent, unwanted, and anxiety provoking.

✓ Compulsions are the repetitive rituals you engage in to get rid of the obsession, to alleviate the anxiety, or to prevent some feared consequence from happening. There is a sense of urgency with the compulsion that feels like you *have to* do it.

✓ A compulsion can also be a value in a different context. If you are ever unsure if the ritual you are doing is a value or a compulsion, ask yourself, *What is the function of this behavior?* Explore the reason you are engaging in it to begin with.

✓ No matter what OCD model you connect to the best, it always ends up in a compulsion. If there were not an obsession, there would not be a compulsion. And if there is a compulsion, there must be an obsession prior to it. Decreasing these compulsions is a vital part of OCD treatment.

Notes

Feel free to use this section to jot down any notes about the content of this chapter. This might be used for additional obsessions and compulsions you want to address, extra space to identify your OCD cycle or obsessional sequence, or even words of encouragement as you begin this journey!

_____

_____

_____

_____

_____

_____

_____

_____

_____

_____

_____

_____

_____

CHAPTER 2

Reassurance Compulsions

Carson has experienced constant intrusive thoughts about his faith for the last year. He doubts and fears that he is offending a higher being, or whether he is engaging in his religious practices in the perfect manner, or that he will be punished one day. He shares with others that he believes he is a good person and practices his faith as he should, but there is a persistent nagging voice that makes him question "but what if…" These intrusive thoughts have become so anxiety provoking, he does anything he can in the moment to make them go away. He tries to feel immediate relief from the anxiety and hopes to prevent anything bad from happening. To do this, he engages in repetitive rituals, including confessing to his priest more than he would typically like to do. He searches online for quizzes, articles, and blogs that will tell him if he is doing enough regarding his faith. Carson also asks his significant other if he is a good person.

Reassurance is the attempt to remove doubt or fear. In that sense, many compulsions are reassurance seeking, as compulsions seek information to provide us relief that nothing bad is going to happen. The most common example of reassurance compulsions is repetitively asking someone questions in an attempt to feel better. This can sound like "Do you think I'm a bad person?" Another common example is repetitively providing ourselves with reassurance. Self-reassurance phrases can vary, but yours might sound like "It will be fine" and "That would never happen."

Reassurance is not inherently a bad thing, though. As you will read about in chapter 4, it can often be a part of your value system and something you genuinely want to engage in. You may truly want to ask a loved one a question or ask for reassurance to gain support. You may engage in self-reassurance as part of a mantra or affirmation to improve your mood. It could even be a method to seek information out of curiosity.

We become concerned when that reassurance seeking becomes a compulsion, as part of an OCD cycle, thus worsening anxiety. It becomes a compulsion when it is repetitive, despite possibly already knowing the answer. It becomes a compulsion when done with a sense of urgency, feeling like you *have* to do this to feel better as opposed to you *wanting* to do this. It is driven by anxiety instead of valued choices. And it becomes a compulsion when your goal is to make an obsession go away, to prevent something bad from happening, or in general, to find relief from anxiety.

Types of Reassurance

While reassurance seeking and self-reassurance are the obvious examples of reassurance compulsions, many other compulsions provide reassurance, too, in different manners. These can include both physical and mental rituals. This section will discuss some of the common ways someone with OCD may seek reassurance. Now, it would be impossible to list all of them, as any behavior could become a compulsion. If you notice that a compulsion you are doing to provide reassurance is not on the list, please jot it down! In addition, circle any of the examples you feel are a compulsion you engage in, so that you can refer back to these notes in future chapters. Reading about and identifying all of your compulsions is helping you gain awareness into your OCD cycle.

Asking for Reassurance from Others

Whether it is of your parent, a significant other, or a stranger online, asking others questions to feel better is the most common form of reassurance. You may ask about the actual obsession itself (for example, "Is this door knob dirty?") or you may ask about the feared consequences ("If I touch that door knob, do you think I'm going to get sick?") or you may even ask a more general question ("Are you okay touching the door knob?" "Do door knobs bother you?"). Circle any of these simple reassurance seeking questions you have engaged in:

- Do you think it's okay to _____?
- Do you think I will be okay?
- Do you think _____ would ever happen?
- Are you sure?
- Am I going to die?
- Do you think that will make me sick?
- Do you think I have cancer?
- Do you love me?

- Do you think I'm a good person?
- Do you think I'm a bad person?
- Do you think I would ever hurt someone?
- Do you think God is mad at me?
- Is that the right choice?
- How do you know?
- Do you think I really have OCD?
- How do you know that's an intrusive thought? Maybe I wanted it.

Now, jot down other common questions you have asked in an attempt to make anxiety or an obsession go away:

_____

_____

_____

_____

As a reminder, asking your loved ones questions is not always harmful. Identify what the function of the behavior is. This will be covered further in chapter 4, in which we differentiate between seeking information versus reassurance. There will be times you genuinely want to ask a question, whether that be for general education, for support, or out of curiosity. This is different from asking a repetitive question every time an obsession pops up.

Your loved ones, support system, and even strangers are easy targets for reassurance seeking. They can then become part of your compulsion simply because they think they are helping. Circle all the potential targets of your reassurance seeking.

- Significant other
- Friends
- Classmates/peers
- Strangers online
- Therapist
- Religious leaders
- Family
- Colleagues/manager
- School staff/teachers
- Social media followers and influencers
- Medical providers

Make note of any other targets of reassurance seeking here, as you will need to know who is involved in order to decrease the behavior. Specific techniques based on these targets are provided in depth in chapters 10 and 11.

_____

_____

_____

Online Reassurance

Asking questions can be in person, via text, and on the phone, but it can also be online. The ability to access the internet anytime and anywhere has made reassurance seeking online more readily available than from our loved ones. Our phones are almost always on, with numerous apps and sites that reach people and information at the touch of a button.

There is also secrecy in reassurance seeking online. You can ask about your scariest obsession anonymously to avoid judgment, shame, and ridicule. In some ways, this has been great for the OCD community to normalize our obsessions and feel less alone. However, for compulsions, it just gives us more opportunities.

Here are a few online reassurance-compulsion examples. Circle the ones that you experience and write down any others you have noticed you do.

- Post questions to your social media platforms

- Looking at others' social media for answers

- Googling questions

- Reading blogs

- Searching for articles

- Taking online quizzes

- Looking at pictures

- Reading WebMD

- Watching videos

- _____

- _____

- _____

Self-Reassurance

Reassurance questions may also turn inward. You may either ask yourself the obsession and answer it or you may repeat a simple reassuring phrase to yourself. Either of these would be considered a mental compulsion, if the conversation is occurring in your head. Self-reassurance could also appear as a behavioral compulsion, if every time you become worried you feel the urge to say out loud something like "Everything is okay, nothing bad will happen." Mental compulsions can feel more difficult to resist, as they feel automatic, like they're not a choice. However, they are still compulsions that you are choosing to do to provide relief. Slowing down the process; noticing the obsession and what you feel urged to do, say, or think; and identifying our common compulsions can increase your awareness of when, where, and what reassurance compulsions you are engaging in.

Circle the statements you have found yourself repeating, while also jotting down your other go-to phrases.

- It's fine.
- I will be okay.
- I'm not going to die.
- That won't make me sick.
- I'm healthy.
- I would never hurt someone.
- God loves me.

- It's okay.
- That would never happen.
- This is just my OCD.
- I don't have cancer.
- I'm not dangerous.
- I'm a good person.

- _____
- _____
- _____

Some of these examples may sound similar to affirmations or mantras to boost one's mood. The difference is the function of the behavior. Compulsions are done with a sense of urgency, driven by anxiety, in an attempt to relieve that anxiety. Affirmations and mantras are done from a place of value.

Statements and Confessions

Do you ever seek reassurance from someone, but not in the form of a question? Maybe you simply make a statement, tell them you had an obsession, share a story, or confess to something you have done or thought of doing. Reassurance seeking compulsions are not always questions. These statements or confessions can be a subtle way of getting reassurance from someone. You may quietly wait for their reaction to see if they are scared or horrified. You may scan the person's facial expressions to see if they remain calm and neutral or become panicked. Or you may hope they will respond to your statement or confession with a reassurance statement like:

- Oh, you're fine.
- That would never happen.
- I've had that same thought before.

- That's not that big of a deal.
- That's silly.
- Don't be worried about that.

It can be easy to overlook statements and confessions as compulsions: "I didn't ask them a question! It's not my fault if they chose to give reassurance." Now, it is true that you may receive reassurance sometimes without seeking it. It happens and it is inevitable. Yet you want to be honest with yourself, if you hope to make progress, about the times you are purposely trying to receive some form of reassurance in this subtle manner.

Staring

Staring can be a compulsion in a lot of different contexts, providing relief by gathering information through our sense of sight. There may be many different goals of the staring compulsion but ultimately the intention behind it is to remove doubt. You may stare at people, objects, your own body, or the surroundings to confirm or disconfirm your doubt. Circle the examples you have experienced before and also write down any other staring compulsions that come to mind.

- Staring at someone's facial expressions to scan for their reaction

- Staring at someone's body language to confirm or disconfirm your fear

- Staring at someone of the same sex to check for arousal

- Staring really closely at locks to figure out if they are really locked

- Staring really closely at appliances or light switches to figure out if they are actually turned off

- Staring at pictures on the wall to make sure they are perfectly lined up

- Staring at yourself in the mirror to evaluate if your eye twitch is still there or has worsened

- Staring at the door knob to identify if it is dirty or clean enough to touch

- Staring at your belly, rising up and down, to confirm you are breathing and alive

- Staring at an email to verify that no mistakes were made

- Staring at your significant other to assess for attraction

- _____

- _____

- _____

- _____

- _____

Checking

There are numerous forms of checking. You may compulsively check to see if items are working, dangerous, or turned on or off. You may also utilize checking to ensure no one has been harmed, that nothing bad happened, and that everything is safe. Checking provides us reassurance by compulsively gathering information that tells us everything is fine.

Circle any of these checking compulsions that apply to you. Be sure to write down any additional checking compulsions you think of, as the list is endless:

- Checking somatic symptoms: taking your pulse, counting your breaths, hyper-focusing on a pain to assess if it is still present
- Checking symptoms on the internet, such as through platforms like WebMD
- Checking somatic symptoms with a device, like a blood pressure cuff, a heart rate monitor, or a pulse oximeter
- Checking your body in a mirror, noticing if there are any changes
- Checking locks, doors, garage door, light switches
- Checking stove, other appliances, hair straightener, iron
- Checking food by smelling or by visually scanning
- Checking expiration dates
- Checking ingredients
- Checking for arousal or attraction
- Checking for mistakes and typos
- Checking for signs that you have or haven't harmed someone or yourself
- Checking if something terrible happened
- Checking your car to see if you hit anyone
- Checking to see if your hands are clean
- Checking old text messages or emails for information

- _____

- _____

- _____

Mental Reviewing

Mental reviewing is a mental compulsion in which you go over information, details, or a memory again and again in your head. Mentally reviewing information or details can provide reassurance by answering questions and removing doubt. Read the following examples, circle any that apply to you, and also write down additional examples:

- Replaying a fight in your head you had with your significant other to determine if you caused any harm

- Mentally reviewing a time when you accidentally upset someone to identify if you are a bad person or not

- Mentally reviewing a past trauma to gather more details that maybe you missed before

- Replaying an incident you had with a manager or coworker to identify if you could possibly get fired

- Mentally reviewing a time when you were almost in an accident, trying to gather details to verify if you hit someone and took off

- Replaying a moment you had with your children to see if you touched them inappropriately

- _____

- _____

- _____

There are a couple important points to know about mental reviewing. It is common to replay situations in our head, whether unintentionally or because you are trying to learn and grow from them. However, we become concerned that mental reviewing crosses over to a compulsion if it is excessive and time consuming—for example, thinking about an email you sent twenty years ago and still wondering if it could get you in trouble today.

It is also important to note that mental reviewing is common with trauma; in this case, it may not be considered a compulsion, but rather a trauma response. Some survivors of different traumas think back over the incident in their head, whether to gather more information to process and heal or to explore if they could have done anything differently. If your obsession and mental reviewing solely focus on a trauma, be sure to get assessed for post-traumatic stress disorder (PTSD) as well. It is possible to have both PTSD and OCD.

List Making

While some may find list making enjoyable and others may consider it a value, excessive list making can become compulsive. Anxiety can urge you to make yet another list in an attempt to feel better: *Now I won't forget!* List making can look like anything from excessive to-do lists to prevent you from ever forgetting something to listing names, dates, or phone numbers.

I have struggled with excessive list making since about college. I am constantly afraid that I will forget something important, whether it is someone's birthday, an important deadline, or a task to complete around the home. However, I am not a forgetful person. I am able to recall all the items on these lists at any given moment. Yet the nagging thought that I will forget something and disappoint someone or fail at something is always there. Now, some lists are fun for me. I enjoy crossing items off a list. These lists are not compulsions and not part of OCD. But to this day, you can find countless lists around me—in my phone, on my computer, on sticky notes, on my desk, in my purse, on a chalkboard, and by my bedside. This is excessive.

Write down any excessive list making you engage in to provide reassurance that you will not forget anything.

_____

_____

_____

Cleaning

Cleaning— hand washing, showering, bathing, brushing teeth, disinfecting, sterilizing, or any attempt to remove a contaminant—is one of the most stereotypical compulsions that is associated with OCD. Cleaning does not seem to be an obvious form of reassurance, as no one is telling you what you want to hear. However, it does provide reassurance—by physically seeing that your hands are clean or seeing the disinfectant spread as you wipe the counter down. But, as you know about compulsions, cleaning provides only temporary relief until the obsession pops up again saying, "But are you really clean?"

What cleaning do you do as part of your reassurance compulsions?

_____

_____

_____

Avoiding

The act of not doing something can actually be a compulsion. Avoidance occurs when you purposefully choose not to do something in hopes of avoiding anxiety. It is understandable; who wants to feel anxious?! So, it may seem like the best answer is to not confront what makes you anxious! This provides reassurance that you are safe because you did not go near or do the scary thing. As you know, though, you may feel safe for a moment, but the anxiety creeps back in eventually. Avoidance can look like:

- Not using kitchen knives because you had a harm obsession

- Turning off the television every time there is a love scene with individuals of the same gender, due to your sexual orientation OCD

- Not driving anymore because of hit-and-run obsessions

- Staying inside your home because you fear contaminants in the outside world

- No longer going to church or praying because you don't want to trigger a religious obsession

- Staying away from your family member because you once had a sexual obsession about them

- Turning off your social media every time something about transgender issues pop up, due to gender-identity obsessions

- Refusing to get married due to relationship obsessions

- Having your spouse change your baby's diaper in fear of sexual thoughts about your baby

- Not going to the doctor due to health obsessions

- Refusing to create a will or plan your funeral because of death obsessions

What have you noticed that you avoid? It could be a person, place, situation, object, or even a thought. Write those down here:

_____

_____

_____

Fixing and Arranging

Moving items to a specific placement can either provide relief from an awful feeling, making it go away temporarily, or reassure you that nothing bad will happen. Some examples of this kind of compulsion include:

- Moving all the items on your desk perpendicular to the wall to remove an uncomfortable feeling

- Having all of your bathroom items lined up perfectly in your drawer so that nothing bad happens

- Arranging the items on your mantel from tallest to shortest

- Making sure your sheets are perfectly tucked in and pillows are lined up correctly so that you do not die in your sleep

What fixing or arranging compulsions have you experienced?

_____

_____

_____

_____

Repeating, Erasing, Redoing

Repeating a task, in an effort to remove any doubt that it was done right or until it feels "just right," may reassure you. This can look like:

- Writing and rewriting an email until it looks perfect

- Repeatedly erasing and redoing your homework until you are reassured it is perfect

- Going in and out of a doorway until it feels right

- Flipping a light switch on and off, numerous times, until you are reassured it will not catch on fire

- Redoing your morning or bedtime routines, over and over again, until you know that nothing bad is going to happen

Circle any of the statements that you have experienced or write down your own repeating and redoing rituals here:

_____

_____

_____

_____

Apologizing

Apologizing, or asking for forgiveness from someone, provides reassurance that you have done nothing wrong. This often happens when you fear you have done something wrong, feel you are a bad person, think you made a mistake, or want reassurance that it was okay if you had a "bad" thought. Not all apologizing is part of your OCD or considered harmful. Identify the times it is feeding your OCD cycle and only providing momentary relief.

Take a look at these examples. Circle any that apply to you, while also writing down any other compulsive apologies you make:

- Apologizing to your loved one because you had a sexual obsession about someone else

- Apologizing to a religious leader for having blasphemous obsessions

- Apologizing to your doctor about your health obsessions

- Apologizing for having harm obsessions about someone

- Apologizing to your therapist for pedophilia obsessions

- _____

- _____

- _____

Intimacy

Have you ever considered how intimacy could be used for reassurance? Especially if you have relationship obsessions, intimacy might be used as an attempt to provide yourself with reassurance. Intimacy can be used excessively to identify if there is still love and attraction present in the relationship. It can be used to explore arousal and sexuality. Intimacy can also be used to investigate your partner's reaction and body language, to confirm or disconfirm your fears.

Have you ever used intimacy to provide reassurance? Jot down those examples here:

_____

_____

_____

_____

_____

Frequently Asked Questions

Is reassurance ever okay? Can I do it without it being a compulsion? Absolutely! Reassurance in itself is not "good" or "bad." Just because cleaning can become a compulsion, this does not mean that all cleaning is a bad thing. Our job is to determine if it has become a compulsion, in which case you know it is not helpful for our recovery.

Reassurance is a way to receive support or information. There will be many times in your life that you seek reassurance or get it accidentally, and it does not impact your OCD or worsen your anxiety.

How can I tell the difference between a reassurance compulsion and genuine reassurance? Notice if your reassurance seeking becomes reptitive; if you seek it even after you already know the answers, and if it is driven by anxiety and your OCD, as opposed to your values. These factors will often help you identify if it is a compulsion.

To identify whether my behavior is compulsive or genuine, I ask myself, *If anxiety didn't exist, would I still be doing this?* If the answer is yes, then it is less likely that this is a reassurance compulsion; rather, it is genuine reassurance. If the answer is no, then that is a clue that OCD is driving this behavior.

Sometimes I get reassurance when I don't seek it. Is that okay and what should I do? This is going to happen. Sometimes you just receive reassurance from loved ones or perhaps online while reading an article. The good news is that you did not purposely seek it out and you cannot always prevent receiving reassurance. Unfortunately, it could fuel your OCD cycle, as you have now received reassurance, which your OCD will latch onto for a moment and may want more of in the future. Because of this, you may have to put boundaries in place to prevent this accidental reassurance. Consider having a conversation with your loved one about what is and isn't helpful with your OCD.

Let me pause for a moment and share an experience I had in graduate school. I had a case of real-event OCD—obsessions surrounding a real event from the past that led to a combination of repetitive, time-consuming compulsions.

One day while driving to class, I turned left onto a highway, and someone decided to run across the road at the same time. As soon as I saw them, I slammed on my brakes while the individual stopped right in front of me. They were facing me, their hands on the hood of my car. I wanted to immediately get out and see if they were okay, but they took off running.

I ended up continuing on to class, but started wondering, Are they okay? What if I killed them? What if the police are looking for me, whether that be for driving away or for murder? While these doubts may have been a normal reaction at first, they became persistent. All day. All night. They became so distressing, I felt the need to make them go away by seeking reassurance.

Here's what I did:

I began excessively staring, looking around, listening, and checking to see if cops were coming.

I checked the online newspaper constantly for any reports of a hit and run.

I read local obituaries to see if anyone passed away from a horrible hit-and-run accident.

If I had a significant other, I probably would have asked them, "What would you have done? Do you think I could still get in trouble for this?" However, I didn't have a significant other at the time. And I was too scared and ashamed to tell anyone.

I recognized that my compulsions were due to OCD. And after many years of treatment, I reached a place where the obsession no longer bothered me and I no longer needed reassurance for it.

EXERCISE: Check off all the reassurance compulsions you have engaged in 1) in the past, or 2) recently.

Past	Recent	
☐	☐	Asking others for reassurance ("Do you think this will happen?")
☐	☐	Providing self-reassurance ("It will be fine.")
☐	☐	Searching online
☐	☐	Reading blogs and articles
☐	☐	Online quizzes
☐	☐	Writing on social media
☐	☐	Checking somatic symptoms (pulse, breathing)
☐	☐	Checking for arousal
☐	☐	Intimacy, to feel better about relationship, attraction, and so forth
☐	☐	Confessing
☐	☐	Making statements and watching for a reaction
☐	☐	Asking for others' opinions
☐	☐	Reading WebMD
☐	☐	Checking locks, appliances, lights
☐	☐	Checking expiration dates
☐	☐	Checking ingredients

Past	Recent	
☐	☐	Mirror checking
☐	☐	Watching or reading OCD videos and books to confirm OCD
☐	☐	Calculating probabilities of bad things happening
☐	☐	Watching or staring for reactions
☐	☐	Mental reviewing
☐	☐	List making
☐	☐	Excessive cleaning
☐	☐	Reading old messages to reassure yourself about a relationship or situation
☐	☐	Checking others' physical appearance for attraction
☐	☐	Checking if aroused or in love while intimate
☐	☐	Comparing your relationship to others

Key Takeaways

✓ Reassurance is the attempt to remove doubt or fear. Many compulsions have a goal of removing doubt, therefore providing reassurance.

✓ The most common forms of reassurance compulsions are reassurance seeking from others and self-reassurance.

✓ Not all reassurance is bad or compulsive.

Notes

Feel free to use this section to jot down any notes about the content of this chapter. This might include the reassurance examples you engage in or whom you involve in your compulsions. Identifying these pieces will help you gain awareness into your OCD cycle and will aid you in eliminating compulsions.

_____

_____

_____

_____

_____

_____

_____

_____

_____

_____

_____

_____

CHAPTER 3

OCD Subtypes and Reassurance

Bradley shares with his therapist that he is having horrible, scary thoughts. He states that he cannot get the image of stabbing someone out of his head. He is so frightened by these thoughts and images. Bradley explains that he would never harm a fly, so he does not understand why he would ever think of something so gruesome. His therapist inquires about what Bradley does to feel better when he has these thoughts and images. Bradley shared that he asks his buddies if they think he could ever hurt anyone, to which they always respond, "Of course not. It's just a thought." He states that if he is not near any friends, he will just repeat to himself, "I'm okay, it's fine, it's only a thought." He has searched online multiple times for articles or quizzes that can tell him if he has the same tendencies as a murderer. He has even checked over his entire body for evidence of an altercation, like scratch marks or bruises.

Obsessions and compulsions come in many forms, and many go assessed incorrectly and mistreated, as they do not fit the "stereotypical mold" that individuals with OCD simply love to clean and organize. It is essential to share examples of the many subtypes of OCD. The more you know about OCD, the better you will be able to advocate for yourself when necessary, and the less you will feel alone. OCD can feel very isolating, as you may be embarrassed to share your obsessions with others in fear of judgment, ridicule, or even punishment.

Identifying your specific subtypes can also be beneficial for reducing compulsions, including reassurance compulsions. Certain OCD subtypes, like harm, sexual, health, or religious obsessions, may be so triggering for you that they lead to additional reassurance seeking. If, for example, your compulsions involve specific people, like a parent, significant other or a child, you could be more likely to seek someone out to provide relief. Take the following example:

Jenna reports having constant fear that she could harm a child, specifically her niece. She knows she would never do so and she understands this is how her OCD presents. Yet she cannot stop thinking about this possibility. She wants the thought to go away so badly that she calls and texts her sister, the mother of her niece, to confess her obsession. She asks her sister, "Do you think I am a bad person? Do you think I would ever hurt her?" Jenna shares that even though her sister always tells her no, she continues to call her once a day to ask her.

Gaining awareness of your subtypes will benefit you as you continue on your journey to recognize reassurance seeking compulsions and implement different strategies to reduce compulsive behaviors. To help you connect obsessions with compulsions, this chapter will discuss OCD subtypes together with how certain obsessions might manifest as compulsions.

As you read through the subtypes, put a check mark next to the ones you are experiencing. Please know that other people have had the same or similar obsessions as you have, and there is treatment available—three evidence-based treatments will be discussed in chapters 7, 8, and 9. And if one of your obsessions does not "fit" into any of the labels, have no fear. There are countless subtypes and labels for OCD. It would be impossible to name them all.

Harm Obsessions

OCD may cause doubt and fear that you could possibly harm someone, either on purpose or accidentally. The content can greatly vary from person to person; however, the ultimate fear is that you may harm someone. Harm obsessions may sound like:

- *What if I grabbed this knife and stabbed my spouse?*

- *What if I'm a mass murderer?*

- *What if I shoot up my workplace?*

- *What if I smother my baby in the middle of the night?*

- *What if I accidentally hit someone with my car?*

- *What if I attack my therapist?*

Someone without OCD or without the knowledge of OCD might see this list and be shocked or alarmed because they were unaware of the complexities of obsessions. You, yourself, might also feel shocked or alarmed because you did not connect your thoughts about harm with OCD. Harm obsessions may cause you to doubt who you are, what you could possibly do, and what your intentions are. Harm obsessions can lead to a variety of reassurance compulsions in an effort not to feel anxious, including asking others for reassurance, self-reassurance, avoiding weapons, checking your body or your surroundings, or seeking reassurance online through articles, quizzes, and social media.

Suicidal and Self-Harm Obsessions

Suicidal and self-harm obsessions fall under the umbrella of harm obsessions. However, I wanted to dedicate a separate section to them for very important reasons. Suicidal obsessions are not the same as suicidal ideation (having thoughts, wishes, or preoccupation with death and suicide); and self-harm obsessions are not the same as true intention to engage in self-harm. Because obsessions are easily confused with true intention, they are often misdiagnosed—yet the distinction between OCD and true suicidality or true self-harm is important, as treatment recommendations are completely different. The difference between them is that individuals with OCD are shocked by the fact that they just had a suicidal or self-harm obsession and continue to exhibit anxiety and distress over the presence of these obsessions. They are surprised and unsure why it popped up, as they have no intention to follow the thought with action. These may sound like:

- *What if I drove off this bridge?*

- *Maybe I could take this blade and just cut myself?*

- *What if I swerved my vehicle into oncoming traffic?*

- *Maybe I could just jump off this building.*

- *What would death feel like?*

For a person with true suicidal ideation or self-harming thoughts, these thoughts are intentional and created. Suicidal and self-harm obsessions tend to result in much reassurance seeking. This sounds like "Do you think I would ever hurt myself? Why am I having these thoughts?" You may ask your loved ones, professionals, or even strangers online to determine if this is OCD, even though you already know the answer. Reassurance breeds more reassurance, as the relief is only short-lived.

Contamination Obsessions

Contamination obsessions are probably the most "known" in the world of OCD. However, you may think this only includes contamination by germs. In fact, contamination OCD can include a variety of contaminants you may not have expected. This includes germs and dirt, but also contaminated food, illnesses, blood, feces, saliva, urine, discharge, cleaning products, asbestos, toxins, radiation, pesticides, and more. There is even a concept called emotional contamination, for which you may fear that something (like an object, a person, a place) has been emotionally contaminated because it came in contact with something "bad" or because a bad situation happened involving that thing. Other contamination obsessions may sound like:

- *Is that door knob dirty?*

- *Did someone put animal products in my vegan dish?*

- *Are these cleaning products full of contaminants?*

- *If I lend her my phone, will it be contaminated?*

- *Is there E. coli on this lettuce?*

- *What if everyone in this waiting room is sick and gets me sick?*

- *What if my backyard has pesticides on the grass?*

- *What if someone's bodily fluids get on me and I'm contaminated?*

- *Is this shirt contaminated because I had a sexual obsession while wearing it last time?*

The most common compulsion we hear about with contamination OCD is excessive cleaning. The excessive cleaning provides reassurance as it relieves the doubt that you are dirty. Cleaning can come in the form of handwashing, showering, or using cleaning products. Reassurance compulsions may also sound like "Do you think that's dirty?" (I have been guilty of that one!) It could also appear as self-reassurance, which could sound like *It's fine, I'll be okay.*

Doubting Obsessions

This category is always an interesting one to describe, as *all* obsessions are a doubt in some sense. These particular doubts are about doubt! Meaning, mistrusting your actions, your memory, your senses, or doubting others and questioning who you really are. To some extent, we have all experienced these doubts before, like *Did I remember to lock the front door?* However, these obsessions become persistent and anxiety provoking, even though you already know the answer.

- *Did I turn off the iron?*

- *Did I remember to close the garage door?*

- *Did I hit someone with my car?*

- *Maybe I forgot to take my medication.*

- *Did I turn that light off?*

- *Is my hair straightener off?*

- *What if I didn't brush my teeth this morning?*

- *Did I lock the door?*

Doubting obsessions tend to include many checking compulsions in order to relieve the doubt. Checking the iron, checking the garage door, checking your car for damage or if there is a dead person in the road. You may even check your body to see if anything is not okay, like any sign of bruises, scratches, or blood. I fell into the checking reassurance trap by texting loved ones, "Is my hair straightener off? Would you go and check for me?" (This habit involved my loved ones in my compulsions, which is called family accommodation. Read more about family accommodations and strategies to minimize them in chapter 10.)

Religious and Scrupulous Obsessions

OCD may also latch onto your faith, morals, ethics, and in general, efforts to be a good person. I put religious and scrupulous obsessions together because they share a core fear of being a "bad person." However, not all scrupulous obsessions are tied to one's faith. Rather, they are general doubts about whether a person has violated some moral or ethical standard. Religious and scrupulous obsessions include:

- *Am I committing a sin?*

- *Am I a bad person?*

- *Did I say my prayer correctly?*

- *Does this go against my faith?*

- *Am I going to heaven or hell?*

- *Am I acting in an ethical manner?*

- *Is God angry with me?*

- *Will God punish me?*

This subtype often goes hand in hand with reassurance compulsions, like asking God for forgiveness, confessing to a religious leader, asking your loved one if you are a bad person, or excessive praying to relieve anxiety.

Sexual Obsessions

Sexual obsessions tend to be some of the most shameful and difficult for clients to share. A couple specific types of sexual obsessions are explored further in the sections to come. Sexual obsessions include doubts related to sex in some manner, whether that be sexual intercourse, sexual attraction, sexual assault, or arousal. It often appears as taboo themes like sex with or arousal by family members, animals, religious figures, someone other than your significant other, or children. These can include thoughts such as:

- *Do I want to have sex with my father?*

- *What if I was attracted to a child?*

- *Am I aroused by my pet?*

- *Did I just get aroused by Jesus?*

- *What if I actually enjoyed that assault?*

It is especially important to remember with sexual obsessions that they are ego-dystonic—you do not want them, nor are you going to act on them. (This is the opposite of ego-syntonic—when something aligns with who we are and want to be.) Due to the shameful and stigmatizing nature of sexual obsessions, individuals may delay seeking treatment and sharing these fears with a therapy provider.

As expected, there is often much reassurance seeking with sexual obsessions, like asking one's therapist, "How do you know I would never really do that?" and "Does arousal mean I am attracted to that individual?" People with sexual obsessions especially turn to the internet for reassurance, because it allows for secrecy and privacy. This looks like asking questions anonymously on forums and blogs, watching every YouTube video about sexual obsessions and OCD, and taking quiz after quiz. It's also common for people with this kind of obsession to hyper-focus on checking if triggers arouse them. They repetitively check their groin, often referred to as groinal or arousal checking.

Pedophilia Obsessions

A moment of vulnerability here. It is always difficult for me to write about pedophile OCD (POCD). Not because it is dangerous or any different from any other OCD theme, but because, in my experience, this theme has the largest stigma of any form of OCD—such a large, shaming stigma that I have seen provider after provider, and influencer after influencer, verbally attacked on different forums while trying to educate on POCD. For the sake of decreasing the stigma surrounding POCD, let's talk about it.

POCD is a specific subsection of sexual obsessions. It involves thoughts or urges surrounding children in a sexual nature, which are highly unwanted and highly distressing. This is not the same as pedophilia. Remember—sexual obsessions go against your values and character. In fact, the premise of OCD diagnostic criteria is that obsessions are unwanted and individuals do not act on them. If people act on their obsessions, they do not have OCD. True pedophiles find enjoyment or sexual pleasure in their thoughts. This is the complete opposite of someone with POCD, who is frightened by the mere idea of pedophilia. Their compulsion is to stop or avoid the thoughts.

With that said, hopefully, I have destigmatized this subtype, or at least helped you feel less alone. POCD obsessions can sound like:

- *What if I was aroused by that child?*

- *Am I attracted to that child?*

- *Am I safe to be around my child/nieces/nephews/students?*

- *What if I have done something inappropriate in the past and don't remember?*

- *Should I have children? What if I do something awful to them?*

Similar to the sexual obsessions, reassurance seeking for POCD tends to be the most common form of compulsions. You may ask others if you would ever harm a child, or do so anonymously online (for fear of prosecution).

Sexual Orientation Obsessions

OCD may cause distressing doubt about one's sexuality, and that includes *any* sexuality. Sexual orientation OCD (SO-OCD) was once referred to as homosexual OCD (HOCD). The OCD community has shifted to the term SO-OCD, as it is inclusive and we now recognize that doubts about sexuality include more than just homosexuality. It is also important to note that SO-OCD is not synonymous with homophobia. Now, don't get me wrong; an individual can have SO-OCD *and* be homophobic, but that does not mean every person is both. The distress that comes from sexual orientation obsessions is from not having certainty about one's sexuality, or from the consequences if that obsessional doubt were true. This differs from homophobia, where there is a dislike, hatred, or prejudice of the sexuality itself.

SO-OCD doubts include:

- *Am I gay? straight? bi?*

- *Am I asexual?*

- *Am I in denial?*

- *What if I am in the wrong marriage due to my sexuality?*

- *What if I never figure it out?*

SO-OCD can include a variety of compulsions, such as arousal checking, checking your attraction, asking for reassurance from your significant other, or taking quizzes on how to determine your sexuality.

Gender Identity Obsessions

As the world has become more informed about gender identity and identifying one's pronouns, this has given OCD a whole new subtype. Gender identity obsessions cause doubt about one's gender or raise the possibility of never knowing your gender for sure. As with sexual orientation OCD, gender identity OCD is not a general curiosity. It is tormenting, nagging thoughts that produce anxiety:

- *Am I really male?*

- *What if I am female?*

- *Maybe I am non-binary.*

- *What if I never really know?*

Gender identity obsessions may be followed by reassurance questions: "How do I know my gender for sure?" "What do *you* think my gender is?" "How would I know?"

Relationship Obsessions

Relationship OCD (ROCD) causes doubt about relationships, sex, and intimacy; however, ROCD goes beyond the general curiosity about if your relationship is working. In fact, your relationship could be perfectly fine, but OCD questions, "But what if it isn't?" ROCD may even go beyond relationships with your significant other. It can include those with family, friends, or colleagues:

- *But are you really happy?*

- *What if I want to cheat on my spouse?*

- *Do I love them enough?*

- *Am I attracted to my spouse? Is that how they want to be kissed and touched?*

- *Am I a good enough friend?*

- *Are they upset with me?*

- *Am I smart enough for them?*

- *How long will we last?*

- *Are they "the one"?*

Reassurance seeking compulsions with ROCD are most often directed at the loved one with questions like "Do you love me?" or "Are we happy?" or "Should we be together?" These constant questions can lead to tension and conflict, which will be further addressed in chapter 10.

Death Obsessions

Who loves talking about death? It is such a taboo and highly avoided topic, which makes it a perfect opportunity for OCD to torment you. While we all think about death to some extent, imagine if you could not stop thinking about death all day long. This is more than simply worrying about a loved one, planning your funeral some day and creating a will, or grieving a loss. Death obsessions are unwanted, time consuming, and distressing. Common thoughts include:

- *When or how will I die?*

- *What happens in the afterlife?*

- *Will I know I'm dead?*

- *What is death like?*

- *Will I suffer?*

- *When will my loved ones die?*

Death obsessions lead to a variety of compulsions, including reassurance seeking, praying, checking physiological symptoms, and avoiding triggers that remind you of death and dying (cemeteries, obituaries, funerals, and so forth).

Existential Obsessions

Death obsessions are about what happens after our reality ends. Existential obsessions take that a step further and doubt our entire existence. They are centered around our meaning, purpose, and reality here on earth. Obsessions include:

- *What is my purpose on earth?*

- *What if all this is just a dream?*

- *Is this all even real?*

- *Am I really here?*

- *Am I already dead?*

In addition to the compulsions named above for death obsessions, I have noticed that many clients research existential obsessions, googling with the hope that somewhere in the World Wide Web, there is a magical answer to their questions.

Symmetry, Exactness, Order Obsessions

This category involves a variety of obsessions about how something is placed. Is it in the correct spot? Is it even? Is it symmetrical? Is it arranged and ordered correctly? You do not want to confuse this with preferences and likes, though. Everybody has their tendencies and likes things organized in a certain way. A preferred organization style does not mean you have OCD. To determine if it might be OCD, ask yourself if organizing is something you like or enjoy, or if it is anxiety provoking. These kinds of obsessions might sound like:

- *Is that picture frame parallel to the floor?*

- *Are the candles lined up from tallest to shortest?*

- *Are the books symmetrical on both sides of the book case?*

- *My closet has to be color coded from black to white.*

- *Are my drawers shut completely before bedtime?*

- *Is everything on my desk facing forward when I leave for the day?*

The number one compulsion seen with this subtype is moving, arranging, and fixing items: tilting the picture frame, lining the candles up, arranging the books to look symmetrical, and so forth.

Just-Right Obsessions

You may also experience situations that fundamentally do not "feel right." There is no specific consequence to these obsessions, like "my dog will drop dead;" rather, this form of OCD is a feeling of tension if something is not "just right." Some of the symmetry, exactness, and order obsessions may also fit into this description:

- *The volume on my television has to be on an even number.*

- *I must flip the light switch on and off until the switch feels right.*

- *I need to step on the ball of my foot just right, otherwise I have to start over.*

- *I have to walk in and out of the doorway until the feeling is right.*

Perfectionism Obsessions

Obsessions that latch onto the smallest detail in hopes of perfection can become time consuming. An email can be reviewed, and reviewed again, and analyzed, as you seek reassurance that it is all okay (even if it's already error free). Perfectionism obsessions involve a lot of fixing, reassurance seeking, and mental reviewing:

- *Did I make a mistake?*
- *Was there a typo in that last email?*
- *What if I'm a minute late?*
- *What if that assignment isn't perfect?*

Postpartum Obsessions

We have all heard of postpartum depression. And some may have even heard of postpartum anxiety. But what about postpartum OCD? These are scary, unwanted, persistent thoughts about your baby. It is especially important to advocate for people with this subtype, as an untrained professional could view these obsessions as a reason to report to child protective services. In fact, these parents are the least likely of any new parents to harm their child in my experience. Punishing someone for their obsessions will ultimately worsen their OCD in the long run, as it just gives their obsession even more power. Postpartum obsessions include:

- *What if I touch my baby inappropriately?*
- *What if I accidentally drop my baby?*
- *What if I smother my baby when they are asleep?*
- *What if someone kidnaps my baby?*
- *What if I roll over on my baby and smother him while snuggling?*
- *What if my baby becomes contaminated?*

These caregivers may excessively check on their bundle of joy—even more than the typical parent does. And if they feel brave enough to talk to an OCD specialist, we may hear questions like "But how do you know I would never hurt my child? Do you think I'm a bad parent?"

Real-Event Obsessions

Real-event OCD throws a new spin on OCD. You typically think of obsessions as "made-up scenarios" or fears about the future. With real-event OCD, obsessions are about actual events that have occurred.

Though the event is real, the story you create about the obsessional doubt is typically not real. Real-event OCD is different from a trauma response, as the event can be a minimal situation, like an email that was sent or a conversation you had with a friend. Here are some examples:

- *What if I could have prevented that?*

- *Did I handle that right?*

- *What if that means I'm a bad person?*

- *Am I remembering that correctly?*

- *Maybe I really meant to do that.*

- *What if I actually hurt them?*

- *Could I still get in trouble for that now?*

- *What if someone still finds out?*

A subset of real-event OCD is false-memory OCD. With false-memory obsessions, you may begin to question if you are making up situations or if you can't remember whether something truly happened. With both themes, you may exhibit mental rituals like replaying the situation in your head to reassure yourself, in hopes of gathering details and solving the obsession.

Sensorimotor Obsessions

We have discussed a lot of obsessions that are thoughts, but they can also be bodily sensations and hyper-focusing on these bodily sensations. This may also be referred to as somatic obsessions, bodily obsessions, or hyper-awareness obsessions. With sensorimotor obsessions, you are not making up the sensation. Your eye really is twitching, you really do have heart palpitations, you really do have a pain in your leg. However, OCD tells you, "Hey, you should pay extra close attention to that sensation and figure it out!" Sensorimotor obsessions include:

- Constantly paying attention to the ringing in your ears

- Hyper-focusing on a twitch in your eye

- Getting stuck on your heart beat

- Hyper-focusing on your breathing

The hyper-focusing, or paying attention to bodily sensations, tends to be the prominent compulsion, in an effort to "figure it out" and bring some relief. However, you may do the opposite, in which you attempt to ignore the sensation. You may also utilize reassurance seeking with medical professionals, excessively enquiring about these sensations.

Meta Obsessions

Meta OCD is obsessions about obsessions, or OCD about OCD. This is when our obsessions latch onto our obsessions, diagnosis, or treatment:

- *Why am I not worried about that thought? Does that mean I like it?*

- *Am I worried enough about that? Should I be worried more?*

- *Am I actually getting better?*

- *I'm feeling better; does that mean I made up my OCD?*

- *Maybe I don't really have OCD.*

- *What if I really did want that thought?*

Meta obsessions are often accompanied by reassurance seeking compulsions. This may sound like "Do you think I actually wanted that thought? What if this one is different? How would you know the difference?"—even though you may already know the answers.

That is a ton of subtypes! Do not panic if your specific obsession does not fit into the perfect box. The category which your obsessions fall under is not important. It is still OCD at the end of the day. Subtypes can simply help with normalization and understanding stigma, in addition to identifying the reassurance compulsions that may follow.

Additional Disorders

The following disorders are not the same as OCD; however, the preoccupation with certain thoughts presents itself similarly to OCD obsessions. If you recognize yourself in any of these examples, make a note of it! Some of the strategies in this workbook can be helpful for any rituals you are engaging in, but additional treatment may also be needed.

Body Dysmorphic Disorder

Body dysmorphic disorder (BDD) is under the umbrella of obsessive-compulsive and related disorders. This disorder involves preoccupation with a perceived physical flaw, or if a flaw does exist, a minimal one. BDD is not the same as OCD, but the obsessions about one's appearance are similar to obsessions:

- *Is my nose crooked?*

- *What if my calves are uneven?*

- *What if my breasts are different sizes?*

- *What if my penis isn't long enough?*

- *What if my face is covered in acne?*

Health Obsessions

Health obsessions are unwanted and distressing thoughts surrounding significant illnesses, which can be a part of OCD or warrant another diagnosis altogether: illness anxiety disorder. These obsessions can widely vary:

- *Is that pain actually cancer?*

- *What if the reason I am forgetting is because I have dementia?*

- *What if that pain never goes away?*

- *Is that eye twitch a sign of a tumor?*

- *What if I die early?*

Panic Disorder

Panic attacks involve a sudden episode with physical sensations and intense fear, often with no trigger. Physical sensations include a racing heart, difficulty breathing, feeling lightheaded, nausea, and shaking, to name a few. A subset of people with panic attacks are diagnosed with panic disorder. They become fearful of having another panic attack, or the consequences of having a panic attack, which can sound like:

- *What if I have a panic attack at the store again?*

- *What if my heart rate speeds up so much, I have a heart attack?*

- *What if I pass out in public and embarrass myself?*

Social Phobia

Social phobia, also referred to as social anxiety, involves a fear of judgment, embarrassment, or public scrutiny. The preoccupation with certain social situations sounds similar to that of obsessions and includes:

- *What if I trip and embarrass myself?*

- *What if everyone is talking about me?*

- *What if I stutter during my presentation and everyone laughs?*

- *Is everybody judging me?*

Emetophobia

Emetophobia is a fear of vomit, vomiting, others vomiting, and being around someone sick who may vomit. It is conceptualized similarly to OCD due to its preoccupations with vomit and compulsive rituals to make the doubt go away. Obsessions include:

- *What if I vomit?*

- *What if I eat something and it makes me nauseous? I could vomit.*

- *What if they're sick and vomit in front of me?*

EXERCISE: Now that we have reviewed some of the common subtypes of OCD, let's identify yours. You may have one common subtype, under which a lot of your obsessions fall. Or you may have a variety of subtypes. There is no right or wrong answer! Take a peek back at your obsessions, identified in chapter 1, plus the items you checked off above. Jot down your common subtypes here:

_____

_____

_____

_____

Have you identified any further reassurance compulsions you engage in? Make note of them here:

_____

_____

_____

_____

_____

Key Takeaways

✓ There are many subtypes, or "flavors," of OCD. At the end of the day, they are all OCD; however, some of these subtypes may lead to more shame and stigmatization than others.

✓ Harm obsessions do not mean you are dangerous or are going to hurt anyone. They are ego-dystonic, as are all obsessions, and are not a characterization of you.

✓ Sexual obsessions are often accompanied by more shame. Keeping these fears to yourself can feel very isolating.

✓ Postpartum obsessions do not mean you are a danger to your child. In fact, you love your child so much, just the thought of harm being done to them scares you.

✓ Other mental health diagnoses generate sticky thoughts similar to OCD. These include panic disorder, social phobia, illness anxiety disorder, body dysmorphic disorder, and emetophobia.

Notes

Feel free to use this section to jot down any notes about the content of this chapter. This might include information about the subtypes you experience, what those obsessions sound like, or the compulsions you experience. If you are experiencing any particular emotions from a subtype— like shame, embarrassment, or sadness—please use this space to share that and provide yourself with self-compassion. You are not alone in this journey.

_____

_____

_____

_____

_____

_____

_____

CHAPTER 4

Information Seeking

Carson is starting to question his faith and the beliefs he was taught as a child. He is recognizing that some of the beliefs that have been ingrained in him conflict with his value of being accepting of all walks of life. Carson decided he would like to explore other religions to see if there is one better suited for his lifestyle. He goes about gathering this information in several different ways. Carson begins reaching out to different churches and religious leaders to ask his most important questions. He also spends about an hour a week at the public library to see what information he can obtain now. In his spare time, he searches online for educational content as well as opinions from loved ones and mentors.

Carson is engaging in a common process called information seeking. This can look similar to reassurance seeking, so it is helpful to understand the difference, as you are not going to eliminate all information seeking from your life. There will be times when you are genuinely seeking information, whether it's at work, about your health, or regarding a number of personal situations. You do not want to confuse information seeking with compulsions as part of your OCD, as you would be missing out on a lot of opportunities to learn throughout your lifetime.

What Is Information Seeking?

Information seeking is a process of gathering information or knowledge. This can be done by asking other people questions, via technology, or through an old-fashioned trip to the library to read books and journals. There are some main differences between information seeking and reassurance seeking (as a compulsion) that can help you distinguish between the two.

Curiosity

Information seeking, as a healthy practice, tends to come from a place of curiosity:

- You notice a red, bumpy rash on your newborn's body and are curious what this could be, so you go on WebMD.

- You want to watch your favorite team's game on television tonight, but are unsure what time they play. So, you ask Alexa.

- You are curious what recipes you could make with avocados, as this is your new favorite food. So, you call your best friend, who is a chef.

Out of curiosity, you might search for this information online, text your best friend, or go to the library. The motivation behind these actions is curiosity or interest.

In contrast, reassurance seeking compulsions are driven by anxiety, as an attempt to relieve that anxiety or fear. Distinguishing between them can be complicated by the fact that sometimes you may seek information with anxiety present as well. I can recall a time that my infant had a cough and I searched for ways to help relieve a baby's cough and congestion. The primary function of looking up how to provide my baby relief was to seek knowledge and alleviate her cold symptoms. Was I also anxious? Yes. The presence of anxiety does not automatically make a behavior a compulsion, hence why you must look at the additional criteria below.

Unknown Information

One helpful way to distinguish between information seeking and reassurance seeking compulsions is to ask yourself a simple question: *Do I already have this information?* We often seek information about information we do not know yet:

- At what temperature do I need to take my toddler to the emergency room?

- How many miles before my car needs an oil change?

- What should the temperature be inside a pot roast before I serve it?

- What is the best way to get a red wine stain out of a white pillow?

If you find yourself looking up the same information over and over again, even though you already know the answer, you may have a compulsion. Or, when you are reassurance seeking, you might already have an answer but are questioning it. With information seeking, you probably don't look up that same information repeatedly unless you forget.

Asking One Time

To piggyback off of the last criterion, information seeking tends to be completed one time. You may seek the information, and then not feel the need to do it again (unless you forget or need to further gather information, such as for a large research project). Some examples of healthy information seeking include:

- I looked up a recent news article about a house fire in my town, one time, to see what part of town the house was in and if it belonged to anyone I knew.

- I searched for the best route to get to the mall, one time. If I forget what route it told me, I may look it up a second time for recall.

- I googled causes of migraines, because I have started having them daily. I do not continue looking up the causes every single day, as I already have the answer.

For reassurance seeking compulsions, looking up information never happens one time. Partially because the definition of a compulsion includes "repetitive rituals" but also because compulsions breed more compulsions. You may intend to ask your spouse one time, "Do you love me?" Doing this provides a moment of relief—your anxiety is whisked away since they said, "Absolutely!" However, one day later, the fear comes back and you feel a need to ask your spouse again. You may also feel like your reassurance kept you safe. It protected you, which reinforces the urge to ask every time the obsession pops up, to keep you safe every single time.

Values

Another way to determine whether an action is part of the OCD cycle: explore if it is a value or is anxiety driven. If you are not in touch with your values, this is a good time to begin exploring this. Jot down some of your values. If you struggle identifying these, ask yourself, *What do I admire or love about myself or others? What characteristics or qualities do I find important?*

_____

_____

_____

_____

_____

Now, you may or may not have written down "information seeking," as that is not often one of the most important values that comes to mind. But is learning, being knowledgeable, knowing how to gather information, important to you? Then it is probably a value.

So, in moments of information or reassurance seeking, ask yourself, *What is the function of this behavior right now? Am I doing this because I genuinely want to know this answer, it is important to me, and it is part of my value system? Or am I looking this up because anxiety and OCD say, "You have to look this up right now or else"?*

EXERCISE: Ask yourself this magical question, *If anxiety or OCD did not exist, what would I be doing right now?* Now, I know I do not have a magic wand to make anxiety or OCD disappear, but you get the idea. If there were no anxiety or OCD, would you still be seeking information? If the answer is yes, you would still seek the information, it is more likely a value. If the answer is no, you would probably not, then that tells you your behavior is probably driven by anxiety and is a possible compulsion.

Let's try this skill now. Think back to the last time you asked someone a question. It could be any question. Maybe it was your doctor about your health, your loved one about a fight you just had, or a stranger online asking where they bought something. Jot down this situation and question here:

_____

_____

_____

Now, ask the magic question: *If anxiety or OCD did not exist, what would I be doing right now?* What is your response? Would you still be seeking the information?

_____

_____

_____

A second tool that can help you identify values: Ask yourself, *When I am ninety years old, looking back on this behavior, is that genuinely what I wanted to do and would I choose to do it again*? I know this may seem odd to picture yourself as an elder reflecting back on your life, but it is sometimes easier to identify values when you put actions in perspective with how you want your end of life to look.

Let's try this exercise now. Pick a behavior you engaged in today, any behavior. It may be about information or reassurance seeking. Or it could be any behavior like showering, working out, speeding through a red light, taking a nap, or yelling at your child. Jot down this behavior here:

_____

Now, ask yourself the question: *When I am ninety years old, looking back on this behavior, is that genuinely what I wanted to do and would I choose to do it again*? Does your answer indicate values or OCD (or the product of an emotion)?

_____

_____

_____

These tools can assist you with identifying what is truly a value and something you want to do, versus when you are doing something only because OCD tells you to. If you are still stuck on if something is a compulsion or a value, chapter 8 discusses values, identifying values, choosing valued behaviors, and other skills that fall under acceptance and commitment therapy.

Information Seeking Examples

Here is a list of examples to increase your understanding and awareness of what information seeking could look like. Feel free to put a check mark next to ones you have experienced, though the specific details might be slightly different. Consider what makes these scenarios information seeking:

1. You have a paper due on Monday for your high school English class. You read the assigned book to write the paper.

2. Your dog starts vomiting in the middle of the night. You search online, one time, what possible causes could be. You see that dietary changes could explain it, and your dog did start a new food today.

3. You are trying out a new restaurant in town. You look up their menu online to make sure there is something you will eat.

4. You text your spouse, "What time will you be home tonight," so that you can have dinner ready.

5. You are out to eat with a group of friends. You are talking about the upcoming election and you ask your friends their thoughts, as you are still undecided.

6. You are getting frustrated with your telephone carrier. So, on Monday, you make some calls to other telephone carriers to find out options and pricing.

7. Your teenager wakes up with a sore throat. You google what would be the best pain reliever for them.

8. You ask your home smart device what the temperature is outside, so you know if you need a jacket.

9. You want to start therapy again for OCD. You make a few calls and send a few emails to different providers in town to find out if they are taking new patients, what their specialties are, and if they take your insurance.

10. You pop a tire while driving. You instinctively call your dad to ask him how to change it.

11. You pull up the local newspaper on your phone in the morning to read the latest headlines.

12. You are in a new town for a conference. You search online for things to do in the evenings.

13. It is your first time flying. You look up TSA's policies surrounding flying and carry-ons so you won't have to throw anything away.

To make things more interesting, all of these information seeking examples above could become reassurance seeking compulsions. Details of the story would look a little different, but it just goes to show that *anything* could become a compulsion depending on the function.

What common information seeking behaviors do you engage in? How do you know these are not compulsions?

_____

_____

_____

_____

Reassurance Seeking Examples

Using the examples from above but changing a few details, here are examples of reassurance seeking compulsions. Feel free to put a check mark next to the examples you have engaged in, though the specific details might be slightly different. Consider what makes these reassurance seeking compulsions:

1. You are assigned a book to read on Monday for your high school English class. You read the assigned book cover to cover multiple times. You are so fearful that you will make a mistake in class, you read through it two more times the night the book is due.

2. Your dog starts vomiting in the middle of the night. You search online what possible causes could be. You see that dietary changes could explain it, and your dog did start a new food today. You feel unsettled, so the next morning you call the veterinarian, who confirms it was probably the dietary changes. The next night, even though your dog is not vomiting anymore, you are still panicked it could happen again. So you search online what possible causes could be.

3. You are trying out a new restaurant in town. You look up their menu online to make sure there is something you will eat because you have a gluten allergy. You find several options that are gluten-free. A few minutes later, you begin to question if you read the menu correctly. Maybe there are ingredients they did not list on the menu. What if you have an allergic reaction in the restaurant, can't breathe, and die? So you read the menu repetitively.

4. You text your spouse, "What time will you be home tonight," so that you can have dinner ready. They tell you between 5:00 and 5:15. At 5:01, you are distressed that they may have gotten in an accident and text again, "What time will you be home?"

5. You are out to eat with a group of friends. You are talking about the upcoming election and you ask your friends their thoughts. You worry you will make the wrong choice and be viewed as a "bad person" if you vote for someone bad. You ask your friends multiple times who they are voting for, why, and how they know for sure that they are making the right choice.

6. You are anxious that your telephone carrier does not have the best reception…and what if you get lost in the woods (even though you never go in the woods)? So on Monday, you call every telephone carrier to find out how good their reception is. You continue to do your research online for the next couple months.

7. Your teenager wakes up with a sore throat. You take him into his pediatrician, who says that it is mononucleosis, and he should rest, drink plenty of fluids, and take acetaminophen as needed for pain. You become obsessed that it could be throat cancer, begin searching online for throat cancer symptoms, and call the pediatrician to see if this is a possibility. When they again confirm it is mononucleosis, you ask for a second opinion.

8. You ask your home smart device if there is a tornado coming even though it is 73 degrees and sunny out. The forecast does not call for storms or thunderstorms. You ask the device multiple times throughout the day to be sure.

9. You want to start therapy again for OCD. You make a few calls and send a few emails to different providers in town. You ask each one, "What if I don't really have OCD? What if I actually become a serial killer?"

10. You pop a tire while driving. You begin to wonder if you accidentally hit someone. You get out and search your car for dents. You look around for dead bodies on the road. You search the newspapers and obituaries when you get home. Weeks later, you still worry if you hit someone and ask your friend if they believe you hit someone.

11. You pull up the local newspaper on your phone in the morning to read the latest headlines. You frantically search to see if there were any robberies in your neighborhood. You are so distressed about the possibility of someone breaking in that you look at the headlines several times a day to see if they have been updated.

12. You are in a new town for a conference. You search the crime rates in the town before you head out to dinner. While the area you are in appears to be safe and no concerns of crime are reported online, you continue to check online for news articles. You also call your spouse to see if they believe you are safe to go out.

13. You have flown a couple times a year for the last ten years. You become fearful every time you fly that you will accidentally or unknowingly pack something that is illegal to have on airplanes, like a gun. You check through your luggage multiple times per day until the day of your flight.

After reviewing this list of reassurance seeking compulsions, I hope you will be even more aware of the differences between information seeking and reassurance seeking, and when reassurance seeking becomes a compulsion. List some of your reassurance seeking compulsions that could easily be confused with valued information seeking. How do you know the difference?

_____

_____

_____

_____

Second Opinions

As with information seeking, the function of seeking second opinions can change from moment to moment. Is it a value or is it a compulsion? Is it information seeking or is it reassurance seeking? Well, it could be either depending on a few factors, which we will discuss here.

Second opinions are often associated with our health and medical decisions. However, you may also seek second opinions on major purchases, estimates for repairs, or big decisions, such as if you should quit your job. In some situations, you may seek a second opinion out of a value for your health because you want another perspective on what treatment approach would be best. Take Annelise:

Annelise has just been diagnosed with stage 1 breast cancer. Her physician referred her to the oncologist at the local hospital. He recommended a partial mastectomy. Annelise was not sure if this was the path she wanted to take and received a second opinion at the hospital in a neighboring city.

In this example, Annelise wanted to make sure she made the best decision for herself and her health. She explored a second opinion so that she could make the most informed decision moving forward. This was not a repetitive behavior; it was not driven by anxiety (even though I am sure she was experiencing much stress); and she was genuinely concerned and curious about what her options were. Let's compare this to Jeffrey:

Jeffrey has grown concerned about his eye twitching. He cannot stop thinking about his eye twitching, is constantly searching online the symptoms of a brain tumor, and hyper-focuses on every bodily sensation. Jeffrey mentions his concerns to his doctor. His doctor reluctantly orders an MRI to appease Jeffrey, even though no additional symptoms of a brain tumor appear to be present. The MRI confirms no signs of a brain tumor. This provides momentary relief for Jeffrey—for about six hours. He then begins to worry that the doctor or MRI missed something. He requests to see another doctor and he insists on another MRI.

As you can see, Jeffrey is exhibiting a reassurance seeking compulsion as opposed to requesting a simple second opinion as part of his value system. Here is where it gets complicated: Jeffrey probably does value his health. So much that it has become a target for obsessions. However, his need to seek reassurance isn't driven by value, it's driven by his anxiety. His compulsion has become a repetitive ritual to seek reassurance, even though he already knows the answer. And I know what you're thinking: "The MRI could have been wrong. It is possible he has a brain tumor. He doesn't know it isn't a brain tumor with 100 percent certainty." Well, you can never have 100 percent certainty, especially when it comes to your health. And he does already have the most reliable answer about his health from a physician and the results of the MRI. Unfortunately, all this does not provide Jeffrey with much relief for long, as he continues to seek more information to attempt to provide that certainty.

Have you ever had to seek a second opinion? Was it a value or a compulsion?

_____

_____

_____

_____

_____

_____

EXERCISE: Here are pairs of examples. In each pair, one would be considered a compulsion while the other would be an example of genuine information seeking. Can you guess which is which? Answers are located at the end of the chapter.

1. A: Betty is paranoid that she has left the garage door open. Even though she heard and saw it lower, she began to question again and again if it closed. This leads her to drive back home and check on the garage door.

    B: Betty has had troubles with her garage door shutting; she presses the button and it does not always lower. She calls the local garage door company to find out possible causes. The garage door company states it is probably a dead battery in the garage door opener.

    A is _____.

    B is _____.

2.   A: Lonnie has a peanut allergy. So, he asks the server at the restaurant if any peanuts might have come in contact with his meal during preparation in the kitchen.

B: Lonnie worries there might be a contaminant in his food, even though he has no allergies. He searches the ingredients on the menu online, he asks the server what is in different dishes, visually checks over the food, and asks his spouse if she believes it is safe to eat.

A is _____.

B is _____.

3.   A: Cassandra is flying on an airplane. There is quite a bit of turbulence. She asks the flight attendant if she knows how long it will last.

B: Cassandra is flying on an airplane. She is so scared the plane will crash that she asks every person she comes in contact with if the airplane is safe. She asks the flight attendant and everyone in her row on the airplane.

A is _____.

B is _____.

4.   A: Penny is completing a project at work and is stuck on the idea that she potentially made a mistake, is going to look incompetent, and will be ridiculed. She asks all of her colleagues, including her manager, if the final project looks okay and if they think she is stupid.

B: Penny is emailing a completed work project to her colleagues and her manager. Penny is unsure if she needs to send it to her manager's supervisor as well. She asks her manager and he states that Penny does not need to include his supervisor.

A is _____.

B is _____.

5.   A: Stephen has had a persistent pain on the lower right side of his abdomen. He calls his doctor to see if it could possibly be appendicitis. His doctor says yes and has him go to urgent care.

B: Stephen notices a pain in his abdomen. It is not strong, nor persistent, and maybe occurs a couple times a year. His physician has found no concerns with his lab work. Stephen continues to message his doctor daily asking if he thinks he has cancer.

A is _____.

B is _____.

Key Takeaways

✓ Information seeking is a helpful process that can be confused with reassurance seeking compulsions. We do not want to take away all information seeking.

✓ One way you can tell the difference between the two is that information seeking tends to come from a place of curiosity as opposed to a sense of urgency.

✓ Information seeking is typically searching for information you do not know yet, as compared to reassurance seeking, for which you sometimes ask something you already know the answer to.

✓ Information seeking tends to be done one time, not repetitively. It also comes from a place of values and how you genuinely want to live your life.

✓ Seeking second opinions regarding your health is a common information seeking behavior; however, it can easily become reassurance seeking depending on the intention.

Notes

Feel free to use this section to jot down any notes about the content of this chapter. This might include how you can tell the difference between your information seeking questions and when it becomes reassurance. It may be helpful to write down the specific reassurance seeking questions you ask.

_____

_____

_____

_____

_____

_____

_____

_____

Answers

1. A is a compulsion (checking, which provides reassurance).

    B is an information seeking behavior.

2. A is an information seeking behavior.

    B is a compulsion (reassurance seeking online, with the waitress, with his spouse, and via visual checking).

3. A is an information seeking behavior.

    B is a compulsion (reassurance seeking by asking questions).

4. A is a compulsion (reassurance seeking from colleagues and boss).

    B is an information seeking behavior.

5. A is an information seeking behavior.

    B is a compulsion (reassurance seeking through messaging).

CHAPTER 5

The Impact of Reassurance and Finding Motivation

Neil shares that he has relationship OCD, a subtype of OCD in which he experiences obsessions about his significant other. While Neil states that they are doing well, he loves her, and nothing is abnormal about their relationship, he is in a constant state of doubt about if she loves him. He states that this is the best relationship he has ever been in, and while his significant other agrees, shows him affection, says she loves him, and provides reassurance, he continues to have this nagging and distressing obsession. He constantly asks her, "Do you love me?" His significant other has grown more and more frustrated over these questions, because no matter how many times she reminds him, he continues to worry.

Neil has become more creative now in his reassurance seeking. He will test her with intimacy, to see if she is still aroused by him. Or Neil will make remarks about other couples and inquire, "I wonder how they actually know they are in love," to assess her answers. His significant other has picked up on these new reassurance compulsions and threatened to end the relationship if he does not stop. Even though she knows his OCD is driving these compulsions, she still reports much frustration.

Neil has stopped involving her in his compulsions, and now seeks reassurance online. He reads blogs about relationship problems, takes quizzes on love, and posts anonymously on different forums. This has taken up an excessive amount of Neil's time, sometimes up to four hours per night. And even when he is not engaging in a compulsion, Neil shares he is not fully present in life and is missing out on a lot of joys and activities that he would like to be doing.

Neil's story shows a realistic idea of the impacts that reassurance compulsions can have on a relationship and on life in general. While compulsions may feel "good" for a moment, they go on to create a vicious cycle of increased anxiety and frustration. Neil noticed that his relationship became tense, his time was consumed by his compulsions, and he experienced difficulty living a valued life, as he was no longer present.

Impacts of Reassurance Compulsions

As you read about the different impacts that reassurance compulsions can have on your life, note which ones you have experienced. These experiences can motivate you to continue with treatment when life gets difficult.

Short-Term Relief, Long-Term Anxiety

Have you ever engaged in a reassurance compulsion, such as asking someone, "Do you think I will be okay?" Your loved one most likely responded with "Yes" or "You are fine" or something similarly reassuring. How did you feel? Most likely you felt relieved. A sense of calm or peace, or a decrease in anxiety. Unfortunately, this relief is temporary.

The relief may last you a day, an hour, or maybe a short little minute. Then the obsession pops back up, saying that something bad is going to happen. The anxiety from that obsession has returned, so you feel the urge to engage in the reassurance compulsion again.

This is a typical cycle for OCD. While you may feel momentary relief, the anxiety always returns. And sometimes it returns bigger and stronger, so you continue to engage in the compulsions.

EXERCISE: Write a recent reassurance compulsion you engaged in. How did it feel immediately after you were reassured? Did you notice a moment of relief?

_____

_____

_____

_____

Did the anxiety ever return? How much time passed before the anxiety returned? Did the anxiety stay the same or did it worsen?

_____

_____

_____

Now let's turn this experience into a motivational strategy. Write a sentence to remind yourself how you can get through this difficult moment, such as "The relief will only be temporary," or "If I continue to engage in this compulsion, the anxiety will continue to return." How can this vicious cycle be turned into a way to motivate yourself in the future?

_____

_____

_____

Worsening of Symptoms and OCD

Engaging in a compulsion sends a message to our brain—"The only way to stay safe is to do this compulsion," or "You have to do this every single time. It's the only way to feel better." Giving in to OCD and completing the compulsion trains your brain to believe that OCD and its obsessions are dangerous. The anxiety and OCD then worsen, as the urge to do the compulsions gets stronger and stronger. We are now convinced that we *have* to do the compulsion. We *must* do it. It's the only way to survive.

The good news is that you can learn to send your brain a new message! And the only way you do this is by decreasing and ultimately eliminating reassurance compulsions. This is what will send a new message to the brain—"Wow, you're not scared of me. You didn't do the compulsion. You can experience and manage anxiety without giving into OCD."

EXERCISE: Have you experienced any obsessions that appeared to get worse or more anxiety provoking the more you engaged in reassurance compulsions?

_____

_____

_____

What message were you sending to your brain when you gave in to a reassurance compulsion? What do you believe you were teaching your brain about these fears?

_____

_____

_____

What new message do you want to send your brain when you begin resisting reassurance seeking compulsions? For example, "I want to teach my brain that obsessions are not dangerous" or "I do not have to give into OCD; my anxiety is a false alarm." What motivational statement can you create from this?

_____

_____

_____

Promotes Avoidance

Avoidance is the enemy of anxiety, as it only encourages you to steer clear of anything that makes you uncomfortable. You may avoid certain places, people, objects, feelings, and thoughts. And it makes sense; avoidance immediately decreases the anxiety you are faced with. As you know though, that anxiety always returns and sometimes becomes even stronger. Avoidance examples include:

- Relationship OCD may tell you to avoid intimacy.

- Harm OCD may tell you not to go around weapons.

- Sexual orientation OCD may tell you to turn the channel when a homosexual love scene comes on.

- Postpartum obsessions may want you to avoid bathing your baby.

- Superstitious obsessions may want you to avoid "unlucky" numbers and objects.

- Contamination OCD may want you to avoid anything that _feels_ dirty, like a countertop, door-knob, or the floor.

These examples of avoidance may feel relieving in the moment, but actually worsen our OCD in the long run, as avoidance tells you, "You can't handle scary thoughts and feelings."

EXERCISE: What has OCD encouraged you to avoid through compulsions? It might be something obvious like a person, place, or object. It might also want you to avoid thoughts and feelings.

_____

_____

_____

What did this avoidance do to you in the long term? Did your OCD or anxiety go away or did it continue on?

_____

_____

_____

Conflict Within Relationships

Reassurance compulsions can cause conflict, tension, and resentment in our relationships. This is a difficult impact to address. Addressing it is not meant to shame or insinuate that you are to blame for having OCD. However, it is important to be realistic, as relationship conflict is a common consequence of reassurance seeking.

Ideally, all of your loved ones would completely understand OCD in and out. They would have all the knowledge and tools on how to support you and not become part of your compulsion and not provide excessive reassurance. Your loved ones would validate your fears, provide encouragement to resist compulsions, and instill confidence in your abilities. Unfortunately, your loved ones are only human and may not have all the resources or support to learn about OCD. Here are some ways that reassurance seeking might impact your relationships:

- A significant other that is excessively asked "Do you love me?" may begin to feel frustrated. This could potentially lead to a separation.

- Your boss, who is constantly asked if you made any mistakes, grows more and more irritated about these questions. This could potentially lead to losing your job.

- A best friend who is texted daily "Do you think my house is going to burn down?" may stop responding to texts. This could potentially lead to losing your best friend.

I don't share these examples as a scare tactic, but as a reality check about the impact that reassurance can have. Conflict from reassurance compulsions is often the driving force that brings someone into therapy for help with their OCD. Please provide yourself with self-compassion and kindness at this moment. Talking about how reassurance compulsions can lead to relationship troubles can feel upsetting, as you might be urged to self-blame for the deterioration of these relationships. Remember: You are now here, working toward recovery. You did not choose to have OCD. Compulsions are not easy to "just stop," and OCD is not your fault. Use this knowledge about how reassurance can impact relationships as encouragement to continue forward.

EXERCISE: Have your reassurance compulsions led to any conflict, whether with a significant other, parent, child, other family member, friend, colleague, manager, therapist, teacher, or stranger online? Please make note of what has happened here.

_____

_____

_____

_____

How can you turn these experiences or conflict into part of your goals with OCD treatment? Are you completing this workbook to improve your relationship with your significant other? Are you taking the first step to improve a work relationship? Describe your goals with OCD and relationships.

_____

_____

_____

_____

Difficulty Remaining Present

Have you ever noticed that when you are sucked into your obsession and engaging in compulsions, you miss out on the present moment? This is one of the unfortunate consequences of getting so consumed by your obsessions and compulsions. Getting stuck in your reassurance compulsions can cause you to miss out on joyful moments with your loved ones. You may not be present in conversations with others because of mental compulsions you are completing in your head. Getting pulled into our reassurance compulsions can also lead to actual danger, as you may be so focused on the compulsion that you miss vital information:

- Checking your rearview mirror compulsively to see if you hit anyone can cause you to not be present while driving, leading to actual danger.

- Excessive reassurance seeking with your significant other can cause you to miss out on important social cues that your significant other is getting frustrated.

- Engaging in constant mental compulsions to relieve anxiety could lead you to not notice actual problems in the present moment, like an alarm going off.

This place where you are no longer in the present moment and instead are living in the imagination is referred to as the OCD bubble, discussed further in chapter 9. When absorbed into the OCD bubble, you may feel like it is keeping you safe, but it is actually making you less safe, since you are no longer present. It ignores reality and says, "Hey, pay attention to your OCD story instead of your senses!"

EXERCISE: Have your compulsions ever pulled you away from the present moment? How so?

_____

_____

_____

_____

What have you missed out on due to not being present? This could include a conversation, an enjoyable television show, an important text, or actual danger.

_____

_____

_____

Remind yourself why it is important to you to remain mindful and present. This could sound something like "I value being present with my loved ones" or "It is important to me to live my life in the moment, not in the future or past."

_____

_____

_____

Wasted Time

Reassurance compulsions are time consuming, sometimes requiring hours per day. If you could add up all the time you have spent on reassurance compulsions, how much time would that be? What could you do with your time instead? Maybe finish that book you have been wanting to read. You could actually go for a walk. You could even spend more time with your children.

EXERCISE: On average, how much time per day do you spend on all your compulsions, including reassurance compulsions?

_____

_____

What would you like to be doing with that time instead? Maybe you are interested in studying a new language or simply going out for a cup of coffee.

_____

_____

_____

_____

_____

Self-Fulfilling Prophecy

Self-fulfilling prophecy is a term used to describe when we predict or expect a certain outcome, and then our behaviors actually lead us to that expected outcome. You may think, _I knew it! I knew this was going to happen!_ but actually you created the outcome through your own behaviors. I point this out not to blame, but rather to help you increase your awareness of the impacts of reassurance compulsions. Take the example below:

Bella is fearful that her significant other, Landon, is going to leave her. She shares that there is no logical reason to believe this, as they are happy and compatible, and enjoy their time together. Yet she cannot get the idea out of her head that Landon is unhappy and will break up with her. This leads to excessive reassurance seeking. Bella asks, "Are you happy?" "Would you ever leave me?" "Remind me why you are with me." In the beginning, Landon is understanding and provides reassurance. After months of this, he becomes more and more frustrated that the reassurance seeking continues despite his attempts to reassure or ignore it. Landon feels helpless, as if he can never do enough to help Bella. He is irritated at the constant need to provide her reassurance when he feels their relationship is healthy. One day, Landon decides he cannot remain in this relationship any longer and breaks up with Bella. Bella thinks, I knew it. I knew he was going to break up with me; however, she has difficulty recognizing that her reassurance compulsions led to this outcome.

You may have experienced similar situations to Bella's, where the obsession you feared actually did occur, but it was because your actions led you to it.

EXERCISE: Have any of your reassurance compulsions ever led to the outcome you feared would happen? Describe that situation.

_____

_____

_____

Please remind yourself that you are not to blame. OCD is to blame. You did not choose to have OCD. However, you have the power to choose whether you engage in reassurance compulsions. Create a reminder or motivational statement to remind yourself of the consequences of your compulsions. This might sound like "These reassurance compulsions feel like they are helping me, but they are not."

_____

_____

_____

Motivation to Change

Now that you have identified the long-term impacts of your reassurance compulsions, you can use this knowledge to increase motivation. Motivational interviewing (MI) techniques (Miller and Rollnick 2012) are provided to prepare you for your journey in part 2. MI has a large research base showing an increase in motivation to make changes for a number of mental and medical diagnoses, including OCD. You will use these strategies throughout your journey to keep you on track and continue with treatment, especially in those moments when you forget why you are putting in this hard work.

Pros and Cons

Let's explore the pros and cons of eliminating reassurance compulsions versus continuing to submit to these compulsions. What are the benefits of eliminating reassurance compulsions? Maybe you will be more present with family, decrease anxiety, or have additional time in your life to engage in values. Jot the pros down here.

_____

_____

_____

What are the cons of eliminating compulsions? It might be hard work. You might get frustrated. You may even fear failure. What do you think?

_____

_____

_____

What are the benefits of not changing and keeping those reassurance compulsions around? This one is harder to answer, but very important. There is a reason why you continue to engage in your reassurance compulsions. That reason is what is keeping them around. Maybe they feel good for a moment and provide temporary relief. Maybe it sounds easier to just give into OCD instead of engaging in treatment. Or you may have never known how to begin to feel better. Really explore the benefits to doing your reassurance compulsions and list them here.

_____

_____

_____

Now, what are the cons of continuing the reassurance compulsions? You may feel exhausted from listening to your OCD. It may be worsening your anxiety in the long run. It may be creating tension with loved ones. Jot down these cons here.

_____

_____

_____

What you just completed was a decisional balance activity to explore the pros and cons of making change as well as the pros and cons of not making any change. Take these responses with you throughout your journey, to keep you on track.

Values to Drive Change

Values are an amazing tool in treatment. They can be used as both a motivator to engage in treatment and the strategy itself to make progress. In chapter 4, you began exploring your values. These are qualities you admire about yourself or others, or the things in life that are most important to you. Remind yourself of some of these values down below.

_____

_____

_____

Now ask yourself, *Do reassurance compulsions fall into my values?* or *Do any of the impacts of my OCD fall into my values?*

_____

_____

_____

Chapter 8 will further explore values as a strategy to reduce your reassurance compulsions.

Your Reasons for Change

Why do you want to make this change?

EXERCISE: Tell me the reasons you would like to eliminate reassurance compulsions. If you get stuck, explore some of the long-term impacts you noted in the above exercises, revisit your pro and con lists, or look over your values.

_____

_____

_____

_____

_____

_____

_____

Next, prioritize those reasons. Tell me the top three reasons for wanting to continue to part 2 and take this journey to eliminate reassurance compulsions.

1. _____

_____

2. _____

_____

3. _____

_____

Find a way to remind yourself of these top three motivators. This might look like:

- Reviewing this page when you are feeling *off*

- Making a copy of this page and taping it to your refrigerator

- Typing your reasons into your phone or taking a picture, so that you can easily look back at your notes or camera roll

- Sharing your reasons with a loved one, so they can support you in difficult times and remind you of why you continue to practice these skills

Motivation Scale

Look at the following scale. From 0 to 10, with 0 meaning "not at all important" and 10 meaning "the most important thing in my life," circle how important it is to you to make this change right now.

0   1   2   3   4   5   6   7   8   9   10

Reflect on this number for a minute. Tell me why you chose the specific number you did.

_____

_____

_____

_____

What might help you increase that number?

_____

_____

_____

The information you identified above is the next step you take to lay the groundwork for part 2 of your journey. These steps, along with the other MI strategies, will ultimately improve your motivation and ability to follow through and provide success. You have indicated a desire for change, whether you are doing this to get back your valued time, improve your relationships, or decrease the amount of anxiety you experience daily (or maybe all of these!). So, continue on this journey with me and start a new way of living with OCD.

My Story

Contamination OCD—my need for constant reassurance over if things are clean, avoidance of touching items, insistence that others avoid touching things—has created conflict for years, both with others and within myself. Other long-term impacts included continued anxiety, more avoidance, and losing precious time with loved ones, including my children and husband, because my mind was so consumed by dirt and germs. It became impossible to remain present with children while my mind was stuck on possible contamination and my compulsions were telling me, "Do something to make this anxiety go away!"

My top three reasons to reduce compulsive behaviors were 1) to improve my relationships, 2) to be present and enjoy the moment, and 3) to decrease anxiety. On a scale from 0 to 10 of how important this change was to make, I chose an 8. The reason it was not lower was because I noticed myself becoming irritable with others due to my anxiety and insisting they engage in the compulsions as I do. One of the pros to making this change was that I hoped I would feel a decrease in anxiety in the long term, which would result in more kindness in my relationships, which is a value of mine. While I am still a work in progress, these motivational strategies keep me going in the right direction.

Key Takeaways

✓ While engaging in compulsions may bring momentary relief, they have many unfortunate long-term impacts. These may include worsening symptoms, prolonged anxiety, increased avoidance, conflict in relationships, wasted time, not being present, and the self-fulfilling prophecy.

✓ MI techniques can increase your motivation for change, making it more likely you will stick with your treatment journey. These might include exploring your reasons for change, identifying the values you want to stick to, exploring the pros and cons of change, and ranking how important this change is for you.

Notes

Use this section to write down any additional notes about how OCD and reassurance compulsions impact your life. This might include any strained relationships from reassurance compulsions, activities and hobbies you would rather be doing instead of your compulsions, and what your life would look like if you had all this time back. These notes will be important for keeping you motivated about your recovery!

_____

_____

_____

_____

_____

_____

_____

_____

_____

_____

PART 2

What Can You Do?

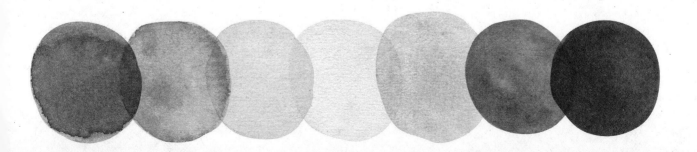

CHAPTER 6

Increase Awareness of Compulsions

Sadie recognizes that her OCD is fueled by reassurance seeking compulsions. Her compulsions appear as asking her parents if they think she is going to die early, searching online for bodily sensations to be on the lookout for, and telling herself, I'm young, I'm healthy, I'm not going to die tonight. This has led to her parents getting increasingly frustrated with her and excessive amounts of time spent on the internet and in her own head.

The tricky part for Sadie is "catching" her reassurance compulsions and becoming more aware of when they are occurring. She often feels like they are automatic. She explains she feels completely unaware of these compulsions until after they are done. Sadie understands her compulsions are a choice in her control, but sometimes it just does not feel like it. So, Sadie implements several strategies to increase her awareness of her reassurance compulsions so that she can then move on to strategies to eliminate them.

Sadie's story is a common one. You are motivated to eliminate your reassurance compulsions that are worsening your OCD; however, you may not always be aware that you are engaging in a compulsion. Before you can move on to strategies to reduce and eliminate your compulsions, you must be able to recognize them first. Explore the following questions and techniques to increase your awareness.

Questions to Identify Compulsions

Sometimes you may be aware you are engaging in some sort of ritual, physical or mental, but you may be unsure if it is a compulsion. Congratulations on noticing the ritual! Now let's go through a few questions you can ask yourself to determine if it is a compulsion, especially one of those tricky reassurance compulsions.

Question 1: Has this behavior become repetitive? If you notice yourself repeating the behavior, then it may be a compulsion. Continue on to question 2.

If it is not repetitive, it is most likely not a compulsion. For example, if you ask a friend one time, "Do you think I should wash my hands after touching raw meat?" out of genuine curiosity and wanting to learn about safety precautions, this is probably not a compulsion. However, if you begin asking your friend this question multiple times, every time you cook together, despite already knowing what her answer is going to be, you may be on to a reassurance compulsion.

Pick a behavior that you think might be a reassurance compulsion. If the behavior is repetitive, how often do you engage in this behavior or how much time does it consume?

_____

_____

_____

If the behavior is not repetitive, then it is probably not a reassurance compulsion. For the sake of practice and gaining awareness, feel free to pick another behavior that may be repetitive.

Question 2: Does this ritual follow an obsession? Compulsions follow obsessions. So, if you identify that you are engaging in a repetitive ritual, ask yourself what obsession or doubt came before this ritual. Is there a fear or a what-if driving this behavior? If yes, move on to question 3.

If not, don't immediately assume there is no obsession. Sometimes it can be difficult to identify why you are doing a certain behavior. Another way to identify an obsession is asking yourself, *If I don't do this ritual, what do I fear may happen?*

If there is still no obsession present, then you may not be engaging in a compulsion. For example, you may do a nightly routine to get ready for bed. You are very specific about it and have a certain order, such as wash face, brush teeth, floss, comb hair, take medication, and lotion body. You may not have any fear or discomfort about not doing this routine or going out of order. It is repetitive because you do it every night—you like having a routine and it helps you remember all the tasks to do before bed. Despite being a repetitive ritual, there does not appear to be an obsession present.

Recall the behavior that you used for question 1.

If you have noticed an obsession before performing the repetitive ritual, what is it?

_____

_____

If the behavior does not follow an obsession, then it is probably not a reassurance compulsion. For the sake of practice and gaining awareness, feel free to pick another behavior that may be repetitive and has an obsession present.

Question 3: Is the goal of the ritual to make the obsession or anxiety go away or prevent some feared consequence from happening? Ask yourself what the function of the ritual is: *Why am I doing this behavior?* The reason behind the ritual will help you distinguish if this is a compulsion or not. If the function behind the ritual is to 1) make the obsession go away, 2) make anxiety go away, or 3) prevent a feared consequence, it is a compulsion.

There may be other reasons you engage in a ritual, such as if it is a value of yours or you enjoy the behavior. For example, Jenna states that she takes quizzes online daily to help her decide what career path will be best for her. While she does have some question about *What career will I be best at?* and while taking quizzes *is* repetitive, Jenna says that she is not distressed and she enjoys taking the quizzes online; it is fun for her. Taking the quizzes online is not a compulsion for Jenna.

Recall the behavior that you used for question 2.

If the goal of the ritual is to make the obsession or anxiety go away or prevent a feared consequence, this ritual is a compulsion. Describe the goal or function of this compulsion:

_____

_____

_____

_____

If the goal of the ritual is not to make the obsession or anxiety go away or prevent a feared consequence, this ritual is probably not a compulsion. Describe what the goal or function of your behavior is, such as a valued behavior:

_____

_____

_____

_____

For the sake of practice and gaining awareness, if you answered no, feel free to pick another possible compulsion.

Question 4: Is this compulsion trying to remove doubt? As a reminder, for our purposes the definition of "reassurance" is removing doubt. So if your compulsion is an attempt to remove doubt, then it is considered a reassurance compulsion. Some are more obvious, such as the intentional reassurance seeking questions we ask our loved ones. Some are a little less obvious, such as staring at a lock to verify that it is indeed locked. Ask yourself, *Is this compulsion attempting to gather information so that I do not have this doubt anymore?*

Think about the compulsion identified in question 3.

If this compulsion provides reassurance and it removes doubt, this is a reassurance compulsion. If this compulsion does not provide reassurance, that is okay. It may not technically be considered a "reassurance compulsion" but it is still a compulsion as part of your OCD and would be helpful to eliminate. Many of the strategies in the following chapters will still be helpful for this compulsion.

Now that you have increased your awareness by identifying when a behavior is a compulsion and when it is not, you may be curious about what to do if you are not even aware that you are engaging in a behavior, if it is done mindlessly, or if you don't notice it until after it is done. Maybe loved ones have pointed it out to you but you did not even recognize that it was occurring. If so, then this next section is for you!

Awareness Training

Awareness training is a process of gaining insight into when you are engaging in a certain behavior, so that you may choose how you would like to respond. This includes increasing your awareness of when you are engaging in reassurance compulsions. In this section, specific techniques will be provided to help you gain this awareness, and there will be activities to help you recognize the warning signs.

Who Is Involved?

Are there certain people you tend to include in your reassurance seeking? This could include asking your spouse if they believe you will die in a car accident tomorrow or texting a friend about your health obsessions. It could be asking your parents if they believe your house will get robbed or confessing to a stranger online to gain reassurance that you are a good person. Identify whom you tend to seek reassurance from, in a compulsive manner.

_____

_____

If there are clear patterns about whom you seek reassurance from, inform them that they are part of your OCD cycle, if you are comfortable doing so. This way, they can support you in your journey, but they also can help identify when you are in the middle of a compulsion and gently bring it to your attention. Share with them what your obsessions are and what the compulsions might look or sound like. Discuss how you would like them to bring behaviors to your attention, such as a code word, signal, or a supportive phrase like "I believe that might be a reassurance compulsion; how can I best help you right now instead of answering it?" More suggestions for how your loved ones can support you are included in chapter 10.

Identifying who is involved in your compulsions also increases your mindfulness when you are speaking with these individuals. You will pay closer attention to these interactions and be more likely to notice if they become part of the OCD cycle. This does not mean every interaction or question you ask someone on this list is a compulsion. However, you will increase your awareness of whether any reassurance compulsions are popping up with that individual.

Your first step, though, is to have the discussion with these supports and explore if they are willing to assist with your treatment. So go ahead, pause and complete this and then continue reading on!

What Do You Ask or Say?

What are the common reassurance questions you ask? If you identify them now, the words coming out of your mouth (or typed in an email or posted on social media or searched for on the internet) will be your warning sign that a reassurance compulsion could possibly be occurring.

For example, a common question I might ask a significant other is "Do you still love me?"

Or a common question I might ask my doctor is "Do you think I have cancer?"

Or a common question I might ask my therapist is "But how do I really know if I have OCD or not? What if I'm just lying to everyone?"

Now it's your turn. What are some of the most common reassurance questions or statements you make?

_____

_____

_____

_____

The next time you say these phrases (or type them or text them or think about them), acknowledge that this is one of your common reassurance questions. Check in with yourself, and the reason you are engaging in this behavior, to identify if it is currently serving as a compulsion.

Where Do Compulsions Happen?

Are there certain locations where you tend to engage in more reassurance compulsions? For example, while lying in bed next to your significant other. In the car while calling your mom. At work with a co-worker. At your desk, searching on the internet. Take a moment to review any patterns of reassurance compulsions and where these tend to happen the most.

_____

_____

_____

_____

_____

_____

Now, when you are in these locations, be mindful of the fact that you are prone to engage in reassurance compulsions there. You will be more on the lookout in those locations and able to identify the compulsion much sooner.

When Do Compulsions Happen?

Have you noticed any patterns regarding the time you engage in reassurance compulsions? There may not be any apparent pattern here, but in case there is, it will be very helpful for you to identify it. For example, do you become more anxious before bedtime, therefore seeking a lot of reassurance before you go to sleep? Or you may wake up extremely anxious and start your day googling for reassurance. Or maybe there is no pattern, and reassurance compulsions happen at any time. So, observe over the next few weeks, and write below any times of the day you engage in more reassurance compulsions.

_____

_____

_____

_____

_____

_____

_____

Use this information going forward, as you will want to implement certain strategies or request more support at certain times of the day.

Triggers

Identifying triggers for our OCD can be one of the most helpful steps in gaining awareness. Obsessions are prompted by a trigger, according to the obsessional sequence. It could be a person, a place, an object, an activity, something we saw on television, something we saw on the internet, a conversation, a memory, a thought, anything:

- A dirty trash can might prompt a contamination obsession
- Changing your infant's diaper can prompt a postpartum obsession
- Walking into a church might prompt a religious obsession
- Using a kitchen knife can prompt a harm obsession

- Seeing an attractive member of the same sex can prompt a sexual orientation obsession
- Intimacy can prompt a relationship obsession

Reflect on your obsessions and what the triggers may be.

_____

_____

_____

_____

_____

_____

Knowing our triggers can give us a heads up that an obsession and compulsion may follow. If you know that kitchen knives trigger harming obsessions and reassurance seeking compulsions, you will be more prepared to resist that urge when you grab that kitchen knife.

How Do You Feel?

The final area to explore in order to improve awareness is what emotions precede your reassurance compulsions, as well as which different emotional states worsen your OCD. Knowing when these emotions are present and the impact they can have on your OCD will help you be on the lookout for reassurance compulsions that may pop up soon after.

Think back to a few of the recent reassurance compulsions you engaged in. What emotions were present, right before the compulsion occurred? For example, were you anxious, and how did you know you were anxious? Were you tearful, and what did that look like?

_____

_____

_____

_____

_____

Have you experienced certain emotions that tend to worsen your OCD? For example, general stress can exacerbate your OCD, making obsessions a little scarier and compulsions a little more difficult to resist. Or, experiencing a difficult day at work and feeling agitated when you come home may lead to an increase in reassurance compulsions because you just don't want to experience any additional stress today. Name these common emotions and experiences.

_____

_____

_____

_____

_____

_____

Notice when these emotions are present. If you observe yourself feeling frustrated, make a mental note that you are more likely to engage in reassurance compulsions to feel better. This will increase your awareness that the urge may appear and provide you the opportunity to resist.

Strategies to Gain Awareness

Now that we know when we are doing the reassurance compulsions, we can track them and notice how often they are occurring. Provided below are several different strategies to track your reassurance compulsions, or any compulsion if you engage in others. Try out a few strategies and see what works best for you!

Simple Tracking Systems

The first strategy is a simple tracking system for when you are on the go, but want to count how many reassurance compulsions you do in a day. Counting these reassurance compulsions brings awareness and also gives you a baseline (how frequently you engage in compulsions now) to document change. You will identify your baseline and track the progress as it decreases every day.

The most common, simplest tracking system is a notepad, a standard little notepad that you can keep with you in your pocket, purse, or backpack. Make a tally mark every time you engage in a reassurance compulsion and add them up at the end of the day.

A simple tracking system that is often used with younger clients is a printed calendar; however, a calendar tracking system can be a great visual for any age. This can be hung in the home, such as on the refrigerator. Every time a reassurance compulsion is observed, you or your loved ones make a tally on the calendar. The marks can be easily added up to see how many compulsions are completed per day.

A final strategy is transferring small objects, like pennies or beans, from one location to another to count them. This could look like having a handful of pennies in your pocket and transferring them to the other pocket throughout the day, every time you engage in a reassurance compulsion. Or having a jar of beans and moving a bean from one jar to another every time you engage in a reassurance compulsion. This will provide an easy way to count completed compulsions at the end of the day.

Do any of these simple tracking systems connect with you? How would you like to go about tracking your compulsions?

_____

_____

_____

_____

_____

_____

Monitoring Forms

Monitoring forms can be used to observe and track the details of our behaviors, including reassurance compulsions. An example form is provided and can also be located at http://www.newharbinger.com/52502. However, you can also create any that suits you. It can be a physical form that is printed out and hung on your fridge. It can be an electronic form that you fill out on your phone or computer.

When you are aware that you have just engaged in a reassurance compulsion, document it on your monitoring form. It may be helpful to create one that can be with you anywhere, anytime, so that it is always available for tracking. Or if needed, fill out your form when you return home or before bed. The only downside to this is that you may forget information if too much time has passed, which is why we encourage using a form that can be near you at all times.

Sample Monitoring Form

Date/ Time	Reassurance Compulsion	Anyone involved?	Location	Triggers	Emotions

For example, here is a completed monitoring form.

Date/ Time	Reassurance Compulsion	Anyone involved?	Location	Triggers	Emotions
Monday 7:30 a.m.	Asked my spouse if I would get in a car accident driving to work.	Spouse	Home (kitchen)	About to leave for work	Anxiety
Monday 8:30 a.m.	Texted my spouse to see if he thought I hit anyone while driving.	Spouse	Work	Finished driving, sat down at desk	Anxiety
Monday 12:00 p.m.	Checked my car for damage	No	Parking lot	About to drive to lunch	Anxiety
Monday 5:15 p.m.	Reassured myself that everything was okay	No	Home (bedroom)	Got home after driving	Anxiety

On the next page is a blank monitoring form. Reflect back on your day. Can you fill out your reassurance compulsions? It is easier to fill the form out in the moment rather than recalling each incident afterwards. So, as an alternative, start monitoring today and complete this form as you go.

Date/Time	Reassurance Compulsion	Anyone involved?	Location	Triggers	Emotions

Reminders

Another common strategy to bring awareness to your compulsions is having reminders to check in with yourself. Reminders can take many forms:

- A sticky note stuck to the mirror, reading "Check in on your OCD"

- A reminder on your phone that goes off every couple hours, saying "Reassurance compulsions"

- Someone in your support network who checks in with you at the end of every day, asking if you engaged in any reassurance compulsions

- Programming your smart home device to ask you, "Have you engaged in any reassurance compulsions lately?"

These reminders can serve several purposes. The reminders themselves will help you recall information to document on your monitoring form if you would like to track your compulsions. The reminders can also improve your mindfulness, bringing your attention back to the moment, helping you become more aware of your behaviors. They can also serve as a source of motivation. Imagine your best friend sending a text once a day, asking how your OCD is going. Knowing they will be texting once per day can increase motivation to do better and better, so that you can share your success with others.

Which reminder system do you prefer? Your phone, a sticky note, your smartwatch, a friend, a smart home device, something else? Make a note here about how you would like to add reminders to your day, to check in with yourself.

_____

_____

Support Systems

The final suggestion to increase awareness includes help from your support system. If you have the fortune of being surrounded by loved ones, friends, colleagues, or others that support your mental health journey, here are strategies you can incorporate. Chapter 10 will go into more detail on how to receive help from your support system in your OCD journey and how to talk to your loved ones about your compulsions, but you can begin using these three quick ideas today.

BRINGING COMPULSIONS TO YOUR ATTENTION

If you are often unaware that you are asking excessive reassurance questions or confessing, among other compulsions, you may need to request some help from your loved ones. Ask if they would be willing to gently and supportively bring the compulsion to your attention by pointing it out. What they say could sound like:

- I know this is scary for you, but I worry that answering that question would make your compulsions worse in the long run.

- Do you think that might be a compulsion? I have confidence in you and know you can get through this.

- I love you and want to be the best support for you. I don't think answering that question would be the best route.

Of course, the statements need to fit your relationship and style, so reword them to whatever feels natural. The key: They should be supportive but they should not engage in or provide reassurance. Decide on what response feels supportive to you and see if your loved one would be willing to help you this way.

CODE WORDS AND SIGNALS

Even if a supportive response is gentle and kind, it can still be frustrating to hear in the beginning of your journey. You may feel shame, frustration, embarrassment, or sadness. If this is the case for you, a code word or signal may be more beneficial. This strategy allows your loved ones to bring the reassurance compulsion to your attention but without an elaborate response. Instead, the two of you pick a code word or signal that cues you that a compulsion is occurring. Examples may include:

- A tap on the shoulder

- Saying a funny word the two of you chose, like "hullaballoo" or "gobbledygook"

- Saying a neutral word like "pineapple"

- A gesture like an "okay" hand signal or tugging at the ear lobe

Whatever the code word or signal you two decide on, be sure you both understand when it should be used. Incorporating humor into treatment, like a funny word or a funny gesture, can help alleviate some of the tension this process causes.

EARLIER STRATEGIES

Last, ask your loved ones to help track your compulsions with the strategies recommended earlier. This might include:

- Have your loved ones fill in the monitoring forms with you.

- Ask the people in your support system to provide reminders to check in with your OCD, whether through a text or email.

- Incorporate your loved one in a simple tracking system, such as making tally marks on a notepad for you.

Key Takeaways

✓ In order to reduce and eliminate your reassurance compulsions, you must be aware of when they are occurring!

✓ When engaging in a repetitive ritual (physical or mental), ask yourself a few questions like:

- Has this become repetitive?
- Is there an obsession present?
- What is the function of this ritual?

✓ If you are unaware of your reassurance compulsions, identify the who, what, where, when, triggers for, and emotions around compulsive behaviors.

✓ In order to increase awareness, try some strategies like a monitoring form, reminders, or a simple tracking system.

Notes

Wonderful job increasing your awareness of your reassurance compulsions! Make any extra notes here, which might include patterns with your reassurance compulsions, examples of your OCD cycle, and what strategies you would like to implement to increase your awareness.

_____

_____

_____

_____

_____

_____

_____

_____

CHAPTER 7

Response Prevention

By now, your awareness surrounding reassurance compulsions has increased and motivation has been established. You are now at the point in your journey to learn the strategies to reduce and eliminate your reassurance compulsions. The most well-known treatment and techniques to eliminate compulsions comes from exposure and response prevention (ERP).

ERP is an evidence-based treatment for OCD (APA 2007). This treatment is a behavioral approach, meaning it focuses on what you do, as opposed to changing how you think about OCD. It is separated into two main components: Exposure is the purposeful confrontation of fears to experience anxiety and habituate to it through consistent practice. Response prevention is finding a more helpful way to respond to OCD and resist the urge to engage in compulsions, ultimately eliminating them.

While this workbook does not focus on the exposure therapy portion of treatment, let's review what this may look like. Exposure allows you to confront the obsessions and fears. The goal of exposure therapy is to experience and sit with the anxiety, allowing it to be there, not pushing it away. Through consistent exposure, our bodies will get used to that unsettled feeling and anxiety will decrease with practice.

Examples of exposures may look like:

- If you had harm-related obsessions in which you were avoiding kitchen knives in fear that you may harm someone, an exposure might be assigned to chop vegetables once per day with kitchen knives.

- If you had death-related obsessions and became triggered by cemeteries, an exposure might be assigned to take a walk through a cemetery.

- If you had a sexual orientation obsession and avoided watching homosexual love scenes on television, an exposure might be to watch a television show portraying a gay couple.

- If you had health obsessions and became panicked at the thought of cancer, an exposure might be saying the word "cancer."

Response prevention focuses on how you respond to OCD. To find relief from OCD and anxiety, you probably engage in compulsions, including reassurance compulsions. These compulsions fuel the OCD cycle and reinforce the fear. It sends a message to your brain saying, "Danger!"

Now, in an ideal world, you would simply eliminate all compulsions, as they reinforce and worsen OCD. However, I like to be realistic and I understand it can be difficult to simply "stop" them. If it were that easy, you would have already stopped all compulsions and treatment would not be needed. Instead, this chapter provides a number of response-prevention strategies to assist with decreasing and eliminating reassurance compulsions. As you read this chapter, take notes to identify what strategies sound of interest to you and which of your reassurance compulsions they may be helpful for. Then choose the strategies that might work for you and try them.

Written Plan

A written plan is a basic strategy to reduce compulsions, in which you develop and document how to respond to compulsions in the moment. It identifies what the feared obsession is and what compulsion you are targeting first. You brainstorm how to respond to the urge to engage in a compulsion. This may include mindfulness to bring your attention back to the moment, delaying the compulsion, undoing it by re-triggering yourself to the fear (exposure), or doing the opposite. These are a few of many ideas you may incorporate into your written plan. These specific techniques are described in the next sections.

The written plan can then be posted in a visible location as a consistent reminder. This may be hanging on your refrigerator, taped to your mirror or folded inside your wallet. Any place that will serve as a reminder, to prepare you and for you to review in the moment.

Here is an example of a written plan I have used for myself, when I am about to ask my spouse for reassurance with contamination OCD.

Name: Amanda

Date: 01/0/1/2022

Target Fear/Obsession: I will become contaminated by touching a trash can.

When my fear/obsessions tell me to: ask my spouse if it is dirty...

I will do this instead: I will delay asking for five minutes, and notice the anxiety

EXERCISE: Let's practice creating a written plan for managing your reassurance compulsion. You can download it at http://www.newharbinger.com/52502 to create your own written plan. First, identify your target fear or the obsession. What do you fear may happen?

_____

_____

_____

What compulsion does your OCD urge you to do?

_____

What can you try instead?

_____

_____

_____

_____

Now, where can you keep this written plan, so it is available and visible?

_____

Now let's explore your options for what you can do instead of giving in to your compulsion to seek reassurance. These are options to consider as you make your written plan.

Delay or Postpone

Imagine you have the urge to ask your significant other, "Do you think I'm going to die in my sleep tonight?" It may seem unbearable to disregard this urge. Instead, I challenge you to delay it. See if you can wait five minutes before you go and ask this question. You can withstand anything, even discomfort, for five minutes.

Following that five minutes, challenge yourself again to see if you can delay for longer. Maybe ten minutes. Maybe a half hour. Just like you would add more and more weight to a barbell to build muscle, you are delaying for longer and longer to increase your ability to allow an urge to be present, noticing any anxiety that is present, without having to give into it.

A few different things may happen during this process. Today you may have only been able to delay for five minutes. But tomorrow you may feel stronger and more confident and are able to delay for thirty minutes. You will continue building up the amount of time until you feel as if you can delay the entire day or week, allowing the anxiety to naturally pass.

Another situation that may occur is that you practice delaying the urge, and eventually you even forget what you were so anxious about to begin with or what you wanted to ask. This is wonderful! Forgetting sends a message to our brain that it must have not been that important to begin with. You begin to feel more confident in yourself, and realize that you do not have to solve or eliminate all anxiety, and it can be temporary.

EXERCISE: Are there any reassurance compulsions that could be delayed? Write below what compulsion that could be.

_____

How long are you willing to delay it by?

_____

If that is successful, how much longer are you willing to delay it by then?

_____

Undo It

Have you ever engaged in a compulsion and you did not realize it, until it had already started or even finished? Then this one's for you.

While compulsions are a choice, in our control, that does not mean you are always aware of the behavior. Sometimes the behavior feels automatic (even if it isn't), especially a mental compulsion. In these situations, undo it!

Imagine the obsession *What if my spouse is cheating on me?* is stuck in your head. You are in a healthy relationship with no concern your spouse ever would cheat; however, the obsession will not stop nagging at you. It would be easy to engage in self-reassurance compulsions by telling yourself, *It's fine* and *He is not cheating. He loves you.* If you already completed the self-reassurance compulsion, then you can utilize a strategy in which you undo the compulsion by re-triggering yourself. I know, it sounds mean, but think of it as another opportunity for exposure—a second chance to *not* do the compulsion!

In the example above, you could re-trigger or engage in a new exposure, such as saying the phrase "Maybe he is cheating." Or watching a movie that showcases an unfaithful couple. Or doodling and coloring a page that says "cheater." Here is a personal example for you:

> *While pregnant, I would experience floaters in my eyes. You know, those little black spots that shift around in your vision. When you try to look at them, they move again. I once overheard someone talking about how these floaters were a sign of a major complication with the pregnancy. I got stuck on these floaters. All day long, I worried about them, trying to "check" them—whether that was focusing on them to see if they were still there or searching online. Sometimes the urge was so strong that I completed the checking compulsion before I even realized I did it. So I had to undo it! I re-triggered myself to the idea that maybe something was wrong with the pregnancy through scripts—an exposure technique where you write out your fear. In fact, I did so much exposure work surrounding the idea that this obsession no longer produced any anxiety.*

EXERCISE: Name a reassurance compulsion that sometimes feels automatic and that you occasionally do not notice until after it has been completed.

_____

What is a way to undo the compulsion? List some ideas on how you could re-trigger yourself to the original fear.

_____

_____

_____

What will you do, instead of the compulsion, once you have re-triggered yourself?

_____

_____

_____

Opposite Action

While CBT is the go-to for OCD treatment, there is a dialectical behavior therapy (DBT) skill developed by Marsha Linehan (2014) that I incorporate at times. It is called *opposite action*, and it encourages you to act in a manner that is in opposition to what you biologically are feeling the urge to do. Here are some examples:

- If you are experiencing sadness, which urges you to stay in bed, opposite action would recommend you to get up. Maybe take a walk. Or get some type of movement in.

- If anger is urging you to yell at your spouse, try speaking in a soft volume instead.

- If anxiety is urging you to avoid cleaning your house because there is too much to do and it is too overwhelming, well, pick up the mop!

- If OCD is urging you to ask your mom if something bad is going to happen, instead you may ask her what she ate for breakfast.

- If OCD is urging you to google all of the possible contaminants on a door knob, instead you will shut your computer, grab that door knob, and walk on out the door anyway.

- If your hit and run OCD is urging you not to drive today…looks like you are going on a drive around the block.

EXERCISE: Identify one reassurance compulsion to practice opposite action with.

_____

What would an opposite action of that urge be?

_____

_____

_____

Stimulus Control

Stimulus control is a CBT strategy in which you make an environmental change to improve your functioning. In applying it to your reassurance compulsions, you will decrease access to or the ability to even physically engage in your compulsion. This might include putting away, hiding, or throwing away items needed to engage in a compulsion or at least making it physically impossible to engage in a compulsion. Or this might include staying out of certain rooms to keep from seeking reassurance from someone or something. Examples of stimulus control include:

- Covering a mirror that you repetitively look in to see if your eye is twitching

- Leaving your phone in another room if you are prone to seek reassurance on social media

- Remaining in your bedroom if your compulsion is to walk by the front door, repeatedly, to stare and make sure the door is locked

- Throwing out the additional hand sanitizers you bought specifically for cleaning compulsions

EXERCISE: Identify one reassurance compulsion to practice stimulus control with.

_____

What environmental change can you make to reduce this compulsion?

_____

_____

_____

Picking Battles

You have probably heard the phrase "Choose your battles wisely." You do not have to confront and eliminate every single compulsion today. Instead, you can tackle one compulsion at a time while acknowledging that you will get to the others at a later time. This can be very helpful if you exhibit multiple compulsions and it feels too overwhelming to eliminate them all.

EXERCISE: One way to determine which compulsion to begin with is to create a hierarchy of compulsions. This means creating a list and ranking them from easiest to hardest to resist. Let's try creating this compulsion hierarchy. On this page, list all your compulsions. Feel free to go back to chapter 2 for all the compulsions you already identified.

Next, rank these compulsions. A simple scale to use is 0 to 10, where 0 means it is the easiest to resist and 10 means it is the hardest to resist. Most likely you will not have any 0s, because if you did, it probably wouldn't even be a compulsion. Write these rankings on the list you made above.

Which compulsions have the lowest rankings?

_____

The compulsion with the lowest ranking can be the one you focus your attention on first, if you would like.

Contingency Management

Contingency management is a fancy way of saying "reward yourself for your effort." There is no shame in rewarding yourself for decreasing your compulsions. Growing up, you were often encouraged to put in hard work by earning a reward, whether that be a sticker, or a prize. While you were rewarded intrinsically for doing your homework, it was quite motivating to earn an extrinsic, or material, reward. Though contingency management systems are often used with children, adults can use them too, especially in treatment.

One important point about reward systems: You will find more success if you reward yourself for "doing" something, as opposed to "not doing" something. What this means is earning a reward for, say, delaying your compulsion or engaging in mindfulness. Unfortunately, reward systems designed for not doing compulsions (having a compulsion-free day) can be unattainable, shaming, and focused on the wrong goal.

EXERCISE: Identify one reassurance compulsion to practice contingency management with. What will you reward yourself for doing?

_____

What reward would you like to earn and how will you earn it? Be specific in what the terms are, such as exactly what you need to do to earn the reward, how often it needs to be done, over what time period, and when you will finally get that reward.

_____

_____

_____

_____

Support

There is no shame in seeking support for your treatment, especially in the beginning. Obviously, therapists and psychiatrists are a huge support, but we are talking about your loved ones right now. Loved ones, including family and friends, can assist by validating our struggles and instilling confidence in you. They can help you identify when you are getting stuck by gently pointing out that you may be engaging in a compulsion. They can also provide encouragement (e.g., praising you for putting stimulus control measures in place) while not becoming part of the problem (i.e., giving the reassurance you are asking for). Chapter 10 will more closely explore the concept of family accommodation, which is when your family (or any loved one) may be becoming part of the compulsion by providing reassurance.

EXERCISE: Identify the most difficult reassurance compulsion you struggle with that you may need support for. Refer back to your compulsion hierarchy created above for examples.

_____

How can you utilize your support system? Can they provide validation when you are struggling? Can they provide encouragement? Can they reduce accommodation, and if so, be sure to read chapter 10.

_____

_____

_____

Mindfulness

Mindfulness is the practice of noticing and acknowledging the present moment. You might notice thoughts that come up, sensations that are present, the activity you were doing, or what you see, hear, taste, smell, and feel around you. So often, we are bringing our attention to the past or future, especially with anxiety. Mindfulness promotes the ability to refocus your attention to the here and now and notice what is actually occurring in front of us. How can mindfulness be used as a response prevention strategy?

Imagine Sarah. Sarah is tormented by the obsession "What if someone is going to break into my house?" This leads to excessive checking of the locks to gain reassurance. In addition, she will often ask her significant other, "Did you check the locks? Do you think everything is going to be alright?"

The next time Sarah has the urge to check locks or ask these reassuring questions, she is going to pause. She is going to acknowledge the obsession, including the anxiety that follows. She is going to acknowledge the urge to check. Instead of giving in to OCD, she will bring her attention back to the moment. Before the OCD cycle began, Sarah was reading her favorite book. So, Sarah returns her attention back to the book: The weight of the book in her hands. The black and white contrast on the pages. The aroma of an old bookstore from flipping through the pages.

Other examples of mindfulness with reassurance compulsions include:

- When your compulsion is to mentally review a past situation, redirect your focus to the present moment, such as what you see, smell, hear, taste, and feel.

- When your compulsion is to ruminate on what could go wrong, redirect your attention back to a valued behavior you were engaging in, such as spending time with your children, working, exercising, reading a good book.

- If compulsions are urging you to problem solve your obsessions (for reassurance that you can handle the bad thing), bring your focus back to the moment and your breath.

EXERCISE: Take a moment to pause and notice your surroundings—everything that is happening in the here and now.

What thoughts are present?

_____

_____

_____

_____

_____

What physical feelings or sensations are present?

_____

_____

_____

_____

What tasks were you engaging in (such as reading this book or doing dishes)?

_____

_____

_____

Describe information from your five senses. What do you see, hear, smell, feel, and taste?

_____

_____

_____

_____

_____

_____

_____

Identify one reassurance compulsion to practice mindfulness with.

_____

Labeling and Abandoning

This technique is typically for mental compulsions, such as providing yourself self-reassurance. You are going to acknowledge and label the mental ritual that is about to occur or already occurred. This sounds like, *That is a self-reassurance compulsion*, or *I am having the urge to reassure myself that nothing bad will happen.* You will then choose to abandon the ritual by engaging in mindfulness or another valued activity instead. (See chapter 8 for more on values-based decisions.)

EXERCISE: Identify one reassurance compulsion to practice labeling and abandoning.

_____

What does the labeling sound like?

_____

When you choose to abandon it, what could you do instead?

_____

_____

So what's next? You have response prevention strategies, but where do you go from here? One option is to use the response prevention strategy you have chosen to target one specific compulsion on your hierarchy at a time. Once you have successfully eliminated this compulsion, you move on to the next.

Another option is to tackle all the compulsions for one specific exposure. For example, Jason is exposing himself to a dirty toilet once per day by sitting near it. Compulsions that typically come up with this trigger are avoidance, visually checking for germs, or asking his mom for reassurance. So, Jason is going to use response prevention strategies to tackle all three of these compulsions. This might include the delaying strategy for his reassurance questions, the opposite action strategy for his checking compulsion, and the undoing strategy for any avoidance.

Implementing the Strategies

Review your notes throughout this chapter, indicating what reassurance compulsions you would like to reduce and the strategies you would like to try. Start with one, preferably the easiest one, which you identified on your compulsion hierarchy under the "Picking Battles" exercise.

Which compulsion are you starting with?

_____

Which response prevention strategy would you like to experiment with, to resist the compulsion?

_____

When you become aware of your urge to engage in a compulsion, attempt to resist this compulsion using the identified strategy. Use your written plan or another visual form to remind yourself of your plan. This could look like:

- Writing out a written plan and hanging it on the refrigerator

- Reminding yourself of your plan on a sticky note, hung on the bathroom mirror

- Putting a daily reminder of your plan on your phone

- Telling your support system of your plan and having someone text you every day with its steps and words of encouragement

- Sending yourself an email so there is a reminder in your inbox every time you open it up

Tracking

It is very helpful to track progress and successes. The reason it is helpful to monitor and track your progress is because you may be more likely to notice the times you "failed," or gave into OCD and its compulsions, as opposed to when you did well! You may forget about all the times you resisted your compulsions, which leads to a shame cycle (a vicious cycle where you notice only when you don't do well, bringing up painful emotions focused on feelings of failure that can impact how you perform). You believe you are not making any progress…when you actually are! In addition, we do not expect perfection with treatment. If you measured success by being 100 percent compulsion free, you could feel very defeated every time you gave in to a compulsion. Compulsions are going to happen. You are human.

Instead, we measure progress by "Did I resist compulsions more times today than I did yesterday?" Are you resisting that urge more and more as every day passes? (Occasional setbacks do occur and are expected in any treatment process.) To gauge how often you resist or submit to a compulsion, you can use a Resists/ Submits Form. "Resists" are when you are able to successfully resist, or go against, your reassurance compulsion and endure the anxiety from your obsession. "Submits" are when you give in to the compulsion. In the exercise to come, make a simple tally mark every time you notice yourself resisting the urge to seek reassurance. And then do a little happy dance! Also make a simple tally mark when you submitted to your OCD and did what it asked. Continue to track for several days or weeks to notice progress and where adjustments need to be made.

A sample form is provided so you can begin tracking. You may also find a blank form at http://www .newharbinger.com/52502. Even if you choose not to use this exact form, you can make little tallies and notes in your phone or on a sticky note to reflect back on it at a later time.

Resists	Submits

After consistently practicing your strategies, reducing compulsions, and tracking your progress, reflect back on this Resists/Submits form. Here are a few questions to reflect back on:

Were you able to increase your resists throughout your practice? That means you resisted more and more over the course of treatment, mastering some of these techniques. If not, do not be hard on yourself. This is a difficult process. More practice may be needed, or maybe a new strategy, or some troubleshooting on what is not working.

How did you stay motivated? Remind yourself why you are using these response prevention strategies. It is easy to feel defeated in any treatment. Ask yourself why you want to make these changes. What are the best reasons for doing this?

How did you remind yourself to practice this daily? It is easy to fall back into old habits. Sometimes the OCD cycle happens so quickly, all of a sudden you are engaging in a compulsion before you realize it. Did you make visual reminders? Did you ask for help from your support system?

How did it feel when you resisted compulsions? I am sure it was anxiety provoking at first, but did it get better or easier? Did you feel proud of yourself?

Key Takeaways

✓ Response prevention is an important component of OCD treatment, as part of the treatment exposure and response prevention.

✓ Response prevention is changing the manner in which we respond to our OCD and its urges. In short, it means resisting the compulsions.

✓ Strategies include a written plan, delaying, undoing it, using opposite action, stimulus control, picking battles, labeling and abandoning, contingency management, utilizing your supports, and practicing mindfulness.

✓ Then the practice begins. Use the Resists/Submits form to monitor and track progress.

Notes

Congratulations on learning so many different strategies! Feel free to jot down additional notes here about strategies that appeal to you, work well for you, or that you would like to implement. Write words of encouragement as you begin this journey, reminding yourself that you are human; mistakes happen but that does not define our success.

_____

_____

_____

_____

_____

_____

_____

_____

_____

_____

_____

_____

CHAPTER 8

Mindfulness and Values

Congratulations on your progress to this point! Your awareness of your reassurance compulsions has increased and you have begun to implement response prevention strategies to reduce the reassurance compulsions. We will now expand on the importance of mindfulness and how it can be easily paired up with a lifestyle of valued behaviors to further eliminate your compulsions.

Acceptance and Commitment Therapy

Mindfulness and values are two of the six core processes of acceptance and commitment therapy (ACT), developed by Dr. Steven C. Hayes (2003). ACT is a type of cognitive behavioral therapy (CBT) that can help you let go of the struggle with obsessions, by allowing them to exist while learning to focus your attention back onto the present moment and engaging in valued behaviors.

Our natural tendency is to push away uncomfortable thoughts and emotions or deny they exist. This might look like trying not to think certain thoughts or feel certain feelings, which only gives those thoughts and feelings more power. Acceptance is allowing these internal struggles to be present. The myth with acceptance is that we are teaching clients to like their thoughts or "just get over them." In actuality, you are learning to have thoughts and let them be present while you commit your actions back to a valued lifestyle. Research shows ACT to be beneficial for a number of conditions and situations (Harris 2006), from OCD and anxiety to chronic pain and substance abuse.

The six core processes in ACT are:

- Acceptance: acknowledging and allowing internal processes (such as thoughts and feelings) to be present, as opposed to changing them, denying them, or pushing them away

- Defusion: creating distance or space between you and your thoughts or feelings so that you can create a different relationship with them

- Contacting the present moment (a.k.a. mindfulness): bringing your attention back to the present moment in a nonjudgmental manner

- Self as context: getting in touch with your "observing self" that notices and observes all thoughts, feelings, senses, and behaviors

- Values: identifying what is important to you and how you want to live your life, to guide your decisions

- Committed action: taking action based on the values identified

While mindfulness and values will be the next focus of your journey, all of these six core processes will be involved in some manner or another. These skills build on each other and can be applied to our overall goal to reduce reassurance compulsions.

Mindfulness

Shifting our attention to the here and now and improving our mindfulness skills are essential parts of your OCD journey. In fact, they are essential components for all experiences and emotions. You will learn to allow thoughts and feelings to be present without needing to push them away through the use of compulsions. When we are acting in the present moment, we are less likely to submit to compulsions.

Explore the following mindfulness activities and observe which you connect with the best. There are many ways to practice mindfulness and none are right or wrong. However, some may feel more helpful or natural for you.

Mindful Activities

My favorite way to practice mindfulness is by doing what I am already doing: a regular activity that is part of my day and incorporating mindful noticing. If you have a busy schedule and the idea of setting aside extra time for practice is overwhelming, then this is the one for you. Remain open-minded as you begin to incorporate mindfulness into your everyday routine. The practice can feel unusual at first if it is new to you, but may eventually be your go-to skill when you're overly anxious.

Here are a couple mindful activity examples you may practice on your journey when addressing anxiety and OCD.

MINDFUL WALK

So often, you may go on a walk and go from point A to point B without really noticing the walk. You may feel so consumed by thoughts and emotions that you miss out on the joy of the present moment. Maybe you are thinking about your to-do list. Maybe you are overcome by worries. Maybe you are replaying a situation that is stressful over and over again in your head.

Instead, practice a mindful walk. This might be a walk from your car in a parking lot to the inside of a grocery store. Or it could be your daily walk in the evening after work or with your children. This time, purposely bring your attention back to the walk.

What do you see on the walk? Take in all the colors around you. Notice any people present. Notice the clouds and what they look like. Look at the different houses in your neighborhood.

What do you feel? Notice the feel of your shoes making contact with the pavement. Feel the breeze against your skin or the temperature of the air. If you are with someone, feel their hand holding yours.

What do you hear? Listen to the leaves rustling. Hear any cars driving, children laughing, or birds tweeting.

What do you smell? Oh, so many smells! The smell of outdoors, whether that be flowers, neighbors' grilling, or bonfires.

And what do you taste? There will not always be an obvious taste. But sometimes you can still taste the mint from your gum earlier. Or the taste of the water you brought with you on the walk.

Just because you bring your attention to the walk, it does not mean that all other clatter in your mind stops. However, when other experiences (thoughts, feelings, or sensations) decide to show up, like *What if I get contaminated from being outdoors*, acknowledge their presence and let them remain while you shift your attention back to what you see. Sometimes you may say, "Hi, thought! Welcome, stay as long as you'd like. But right now, I'm walking." And sometimes you just picture that thought on a cloud in the sky and notice it float on by, naturally, without having to do anything to make it go away. It naturally moves on by.

MINDFUL LAUNDRY

You may be thinking, *Ew, laundry, I hate doing laundry! Why would I want to practice with my laundry?* Exactly! This is why mindful laundry may be a beneficial activity to practice with. It is a task all of us have to do a few times a week. It is often a mindless task, meaning you are rarely present while doing laundry. And the act of laundry can be so stressful that you want to avoid it.

Use laundry as an opportunity to be mindful for ten minutes, getting in touch with the little joys of the moment: Notice the colors and textures of the fabric—some faded, some still bright. Notice the beauty of the clothes. Maybe there are tiny baby socks that bring you joy. Maybe a favorite t-shirt you received at a memorable event sparks some memories. Notice the nicely stacked piles and creases in clothes as you fold.

Touch the clothing—glide your hands across the fabric as you fold. Take in the feel of the clothing—some rough, some smooth, some silky.

Take in the smell of the freshly laundered clothes. The smell of laundry detergent may bring you peace or relaxation.

For a few minutes, everything is okay in your day as you notice the laundry. For a few minutes, no compulsions are taking over.

EXERCISE: Identify one task you already engage in as part of your routine: brushing your teeth, walking the dog, doing the dishes, opening the mail, washing your face, showering, having a conversation with a loved one, or another routine activity.

In the next couple days, fully immerse yourself in that activity. Notice everything happening in that moment. Bring your attention to your senses and what is happening in front of you. If a thought tries to pull you away (and it will!), acknowledge the thought is there. Don't try to deny its existence; instead, notice that, too, and allow it to stay while you come back to the activity.

What mindful activity are you choosing to practice?

_____

Jot down your experience with this mindful activity here:

_____

_____

_____

_____

MINDFUL EATING

Have you ever eaten so fast or mindlessly that you barely even noticed the food? Whether that be the taste, the texture, or the feeling of being full, it is easy to miss out on this moment due to anxiety. Overwhelming obsessions and endless compulsions can take over this simple act. Practice redirecting your attention back to the food and the act of chewing it while letting these urges exist.

EXERCISE: Pick a bite of food. Something small, like a raisin, a piece of chocolate, an almond, a cheese cube. Typically, how long would it take you to eat it? Maybe twenty seconds. Let's slow down the process and really notice this bite.

Before even placing it in your mouth, just observe it. Notice what it feels like between your fingers. Observe any colors or textures. Then notice the smell if there is one. Maybe it smells sweet, fruity, sour. Then place it on your tongue. Without even biting into it, just feel it on your tongue. The weight of it on your tongue. The texture. The taste. Some foods may already begin melting or dissolving just by being on your tongue, like chocolate. Let it melt. Notice how it melts away, how it feels and how it tastes. Some foods may need to be chewed. Slowly take a bite. Take in the taste, smell, and feel of biting it. Continue, slowly, observing this whole process until every last morsel is gone.

How did this experience differ from how you usually eat this food? Now, it is not expected that you will eat mindfully every single bite of every meal, every day, as that would take hours for a meal. However, challenge yourself to do a few (if not more) mindful bites every day. Especially if you are experiencing anxiety from your OCD or the urge to engage in a reassurance compulsion, bring your attention to a small piece of food.

Describe this experience for you.

_____

_____

_____

How could this help out your OCD?

_____

_____

_____

BODY SCAN

If a mindful activity or mindful eating is not your cup of tea, here is a mindfulness activity that requires no movement or items; you can just stay where you are right now, even if it is lying down. A body scan is a mindful observing of your body, sensations, or any experiences you are noticing from head to toe. We are not hyper-focusing on any one area, rather nonjudgmentally and casually noticing all sensations in your body. This technique may be especially helpful if your obsession is health or body related. Your compulsion may be to hyper-focus on your body or avoid noticing your body. The mindful body scan is like an opposite action for this hyper-focusing or avoiding.

EXERCISE: After reading through the instructions, close your eyes, if you feel comfortable doing so, to walk through this activity. You may leave them open if you would rather. Imagine your body being scanned, similar to being in an MRI or metal detector, from head to toe. Picture this beam or sensor slowly moving from the top of your head. As this sensor goes down, observe any sensations. This could be a pain, a pressure, a twitch, a tingling, an itch. Whatever the sensation is, acknowledge it. This might sound like _I notice a twitch in my eye_, _I observe a pain in my right arm_, or _Hello, itch on my nose_. The sensor continues on down, from your head, neck, shoulders, chest, arms, stomach, and so forth.

Be sure not to stop on the sensation for long. The sensor continues to move down. If your attention turns to any other thoughts, acknowledge what is popping up, and intentionally bring your attention back to the body scan. If your mind begins creating a story about the sensations, acknowledge this story your mind is creating.

What did you notice? Any sensations? Any thoughts trying to pull you away? Any obsessions that got stuck? Any compulsions you felt urged to do?

_____

_____

_____

How was this experience for you? Could this mindfulness activity help on your OCD journey?

_____

_____

_____

_____

Mindful Thoughts

In a sense, you have been mindful of thoughts throughout all of the previous exercises. Noticing thoughts appear, acknowledging them, and letting them drift off. Now that you've had some practice with mindfulness while doing certain activities, we will practice mindfulness specifically surrounding our thoughts, which is actually more challenging.

The scene we are going to create in your imagination can vary to whatever pleases you: clouds floating by, leaves on a stream passing by, cars driving along a road, butterflies flying by, water dripping down a sink. You are going to imagine your thoughts on those clouds, leaves, car, butterflies, water droplets, or whatever you choose. These thoughts will be noticed, observed casually, acknowledged, and allowed to remain as they naturally pass. When you are ready, read through these instructions, then close your eyes, if comfortable, and practice.

EXERCISE: Imagine yourself lying in a field of grass, staring up at the sky, full of clouds. Picture the thoughts that are popping up right now, written on these clouds. If you have a thought like *This is weird,* imagine that statement written on a cloud. If you have a thought, *I'm getting kind of sleepy,* imagine that statement written on another cloud. Maybe an obsession comes up during this exercise saying, *Is my significant other "the one"?* Put that on a cloud too.

As you notice these thoughts as clouds in the sky, casually observe them. This means you see it, without effort, but do not spend much time on it or give it too much attention. Acknowledge the cloud. This might sound like *Hey cloud, I see you* or *There's that thought floating by.* This means that you recognize its existence as opposed to pretending or denying it is there. Practice the idea of acceptance and allow the thoughts as clouds to be there. Don't try to stop the thoughts. Don't try to solve them. Rather, let them be there and bring your attention back to watching the clouds as they float on by. These clouds will naturally float by if you allow them to. We do not need to hurry them along. We can peacefully lie in the field, watching them move along.

What was that experience like for you? Was it easy or difficult to allow your thoughts to pass by? Did you notice any obsessions on the clouds? Did you feel any urges to engage in compulsions during this exercise? Were you able to acknowledge those while bringing your attention back to the clouds floating by?

_____

_____

_____

_____

Now that you have practiced several mindfulness techniques, was there one you preferred? Which could you see being the most beneficial when feeling the urge to engage in compulsions?

_____

_____

Values

Values are standards that we want to live by or things of importance to us. This could include characteristics about yourself. It could be people that you value. It might be things in which you would like to accomplish in life. One of the most helpful strategies in the reduction of reassurance compulsions is to bring your attention back to your values. To do this, you must first identify those values.

You successfully did some of this work in chapter 4, as you identified your values when differentiating between reassurance compulsions and information seeking. To begin, review the exercises in chapter 4 regarding values and list some of the values you already identified:

_____

_____

_____

_____

Values Identification

To identify values you may not have named earlier, here are a couple final exercises.

VALUES CHECKLIST

Take a peek at the list of values below. Some are qualities and some are aspects of life you hope to obtain or you find important. This list is not exhaustive, as it would be impossible to include every quality people strive to be and have. However, we have included many common ones. Circle any qualities you are proud of having or that you hope to be.

Achievement	Faith	Love
Accountability	Family	Loyalty
Adventurous	Generosity	Open-minded
Assertive	Happiness	Parenting
Authentic	Hardworking	Patriotism
Career	Health	Positivity
Community	Honesty	Productivity
Compassion	Humor	Purpose
Confidence	Independence	Relationships
Courage	Integrity	Respect
Creativity	Intelligence	Responsible
Dependability	Joy	Service
Empathy	Kindness	Tolerance
Equality	Leadership	Travel
Ethical	Learning	Trustworthy

Are there any other qualities not included on this value checklist you would like to add?

_____

_____

FUTURE FUNERAL

If you are like most people, you do not enjoy thinking about your funeral. But for the purpose of this exercise, let's go there if you are comfortable. Close your eyes and imagine your loved ones gathering for your funeral.

When your loved ones give their eulogy, or speech, how do you hope they describe you? What were they most proud of about you? What achievements do they point out?

_____

_____

_____

_____

_____

_____

_____

As your loved ones gather and have conversations with each other, what do you hope they say about you?

_____

_____

_____

_____

_____

_____

Valued Behaviors

As you increase your awareness of your values, now we must turn those into actions and demonstrate how to use these actions to reduce reassurance compulsions. You have identified multiple values—those listed in chapter 4, those on the values list, and those revealed by how you hope others remember you. For the sake of practice and time, attempt to narrow down this list to your top ten. List those here:

1. _____   6. _____

2. _____   7. _____

3. _____   8. _____

4. _____   9. _____

5. _____   10. _____

You will be using those top ten values to identify what your "valued behaviors" look like. A valued behavior is an action, or what you do, to lead yourself toward that value. These behaviors can be as small as saying a positive affirmation in the morning, or as big as volunteering at the local rescue mission. Here are a few examples of my values and possible valued behaviors to represent that value and how to achieve it:

Value	Valued Behavior
Adventure	Go for a hike, look up places to zipline, drive to a new town
Career	Respond to work emails, return voicemails, read a journal article
Community	Meeting with our neighborhood social committee, volunteer
Family	Play a game with my children, give them hugs and kisses
Friendships	Text a friend I have not seen in a while, schedule a coffee date
Intelligence	Read a chapter in a book, watch a documentary
Love	Date night with my husband, give him a shoulder massage
Music	Play piano for a few minutes, listen to my favorite songs
Service	Create a social media post to help others, speak at a local workshop
Travel	Look up vacation destinations, plan attractions for our next trip

Reading through these examples, you will notice that some behaviors to help me live a values-based lifestyle are small (like sending a text) and some are big (like volunteering). You can break down those bigger tasks into smaller, more doable steps. For example, smaller steps in volunteering are doing internet research, making a phone call or visiting the site. Begin brainstorming what a valued behavior might look like for your top ten values.

Value	Valued Behavior

EXERCISE: Today when you notice the urge to engage in a compulsion, choose a valued behavior instead. You may use the ideas identified above or you may choose a different one at that moment. Allow the anxiety to be present. Notice the urge to engage in a reassurance compulsion. Then redirect your attention back onto this value. This is how you genuinely want to live your life after all; not living according to OCD's rules. Once complete, reflect on the following questions:

What reassurance compulsion did you feel the urge to do? What valued behavior did you choose to do instead?

_____

_____

_____

Was this difficult or easy? How was your anxiety throughout the process? How do you feel now that you successfully resisted the compulsion and chosen to live a values-based lifestyle in that moment?

_____

_____

_____

_____

_____

Key Takeaways

✓ Contacting the present moment (or mindfulness) and values are two components of acceptance and commitment therapy.

✓ Mindful activities, mindful eating, body scans, and mindful thoughts are techniques to bring your attention back to the present moment when obsessions are emerging and you feel the urge to engage in a reassurance compulsion.

✓ Identifying your values can be a helpful way to resist compulsions, by redirecting your attention onto a value instead. You can do this by reviewing a list of possible values or by thinking back on your life and what you want to be remembered for. Explore what valued behaviors look like for these values and choose to engage in these instead of OCD's urges.

Notes

As you continue to practice your mindfulness skills and live a values-based lifestyle, make any notes here. Jot down your experiences: what went well, how did you feel, and what would you like to incorporate more of in your journey. Mindfulness and values-based living are concepts you will apply the rest of your life, in multiple different areas. Provide words of encouragement to continue this practice and journey here!

_____

_____

_____

_____

_____

_____

_____

CHAPTER 9

The OCD Bubble

At this point you have practiced a variety of techniques to decrease your reassurance compulsions. This has included response prevention strategies, mindfulness skills, and values-based work. If you are still having difficulty resisting some sneaky reassurance compulsions, the concept of the OCD bubble may help eliminate any last urges.

The OCD bubble is a concept from Dr. Kieron O'Connor and Dr. Frederick Aardema (2012) and their treatment, inference-based cognitive behavioral therapy (I-CBT). I-CBT is a cognitive treatment shown to be effective for OCD that resolves inferential confusion. Inferential confusion occurs when you mistake an imagined possibility for a real possibility. I-CBT theorizes that obsessions, those sticky thoughts, are not so random at all. Instead, these obsessions, or obsessional doubts, are inferences, or conclusions you have reached through evidence and reasoning.

The OCD bubble is the place where you no longer trust yourself, your senses, or reality. The bubble is where OCD lives and imagination takes over. To better understand the OCD bubble, you will identify the reasoning behind your obsessional doubt and the scary story your OCD is telling you. These steps will assist you in pulling yourself out of the OCD bubble, or never entering it to begin with.

Reasons and Logic

If you will recall from the very first chapter of this workbook, you identified your obsessional sequence, which is a way to conceptualize OCD, per I-CBT. As a quick reminder, here is the example of the obsessional sequence (Rebecca in church) from chapter 1.

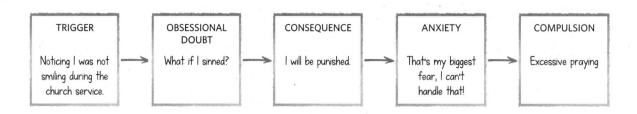

EXERCISE: Pick an obsession that continues to bother you and leads to reassurance compulsions. You will practice with this example throughout this chapter, and if you'd like even more practice, you can download a copy of this sequence at http://www.newharbinger.com/52502. Write this obsession under "obsessional doubt."

Identify the trigger that came right before this obsession and write this under "trigger." Triggers can be a situation, a person, an object, a thought, a sensation in your body, practically anything.

Ask yourself, *What would the consequence of that obsessional doubt be? What would happen if it came true?* Write this down under "consequence." There may be several consequences.

Next, identify the anxiety behind this consequence. Ask yourself, *What would be so bad if that consequence actually happened? What would that mean for me if it all came true?* Write down these responses under "anxiety."

Last, what compulsions, including reassurance compulsions, do you feel the urge to do as a result of that anxiety. Write these down under "compulsion."

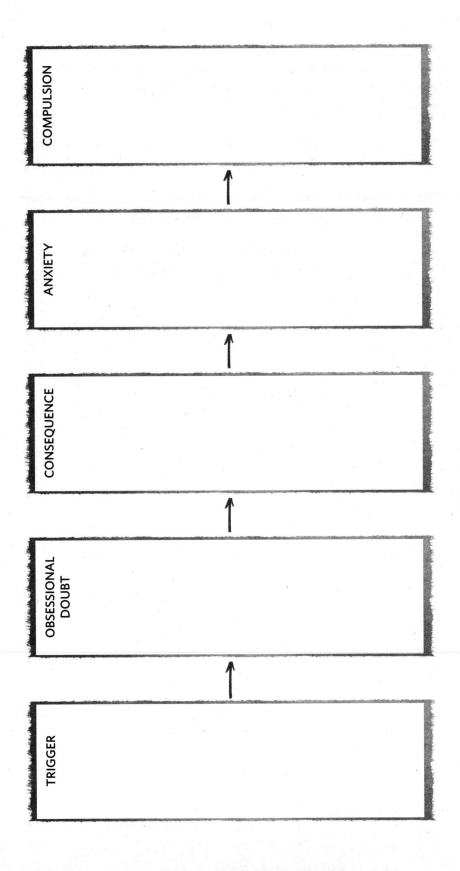

Now that your obsessional sequence is identified, you will explore the reasoning behind your obsessional doubt. These reasons make up the obsessional story you will later identify. This story is causing your obsession to feel so credible and scary that you get pulled in and feel the need to do the reassurance compulsions.

Here are five categories of reasons that comprise your obsessional story. These are 1) personal experiences, 2) hearsay, 3) facts, 4) rules, and 5) possibility:

- Personal experiences include any situations you have encountered that could give this obsessional doubt any credibility.

- Hearsay includes situations that have happened to others you have heard about.

- Facts include any information you know to be true that pertains to this obsession, which makes your obsession feel even more possible or real.

- Rules are standards by which you live, whether they are rules you have been taught in your family or societal expectations or arbitrary rules you may have made up for yourself.

- Possibility includes the mere fact that anything is possible (OCD is probably using that in its reasoning).

To better understand these categories and how to identify the reasoning behind your obsessional doubt, take the example obsession of *What if I get dirty standing over a trash can*:

- **Personal experiences:** I have touched the trash can many times and wound up with something gross on my hands. I have gotten sick many times from airborne germs, like the flu.

- **Hearsay:** I once heard a story where someone got sick after being around garbage.

- **Facts:** Germs exist. Germs can be airborne. Germs are invisible. The trash can has germs.

- **Rules:** We are supposed to be cautious around dirty things. We are taught to wash our hands if dirty. We are taught not to breathe in airborne germs, such as if someone has the flu or Covid.

- **Possibility:** It is possible that the germs in the trashcan can be airborne and contaminate me.

Together, these reasons make up an obsessional story. This story is so elaborate and convincing, it is understandable why someone might get sucked in and engage in compulsions. You may not always be able to identify reasons in every category but do your best to brainstorm all the evidence that makes your obsession feel so believable. Now let's begin exploring the reasoning behind your obsession.

EXERCISE: What personal experiences do you have that make your obsession feel credible? Do you have anything from your past that OCD is using as possible "evidence" to make it seem that your obsession is possible? These past experiences might not be the exact situation as your obsessional doubt, but maybe they are something related or close to it.

_____

_____

_____

_____

_____

Explore hearsay examples next. Have you heard any stories about others that make your obsession feel credible? This could be a situation that happened to a friend, maybe something you heard on the news, or an article you read online.

_____

_____

_____

_____

List all the facts that pertain to your obsession that make it feel real and possible. Facts might sound like "Germs do exist," "Accidents do happen," "Everyone does eventually die," "People get cancer," or "People do go to jail."

_____

_____

_____

_____

Are there any rules surrounding your obsession that make it credible? These might be rules you are taught in the church, school, your family, work, society, or so on. Rules could sound like "We are supposed to wash our hands if they are dirty," "We are supposed to go to the doctor to make sure we are healthy," or "We are supposed to follow the law so we don't go to jail."

_____

_____

_____

_____

_____

Last, does your OCD include *possibility* as one of the reasons that your obsession could be true? "It is possible I have germs on me." "It is possible I have cancer." "It is possible that I get in an accident on the way to work." "It is possible I could be gay." List these possibilities here.

_____

_____

_____

_____

_____

Obsessional Story

As you can see, there are a lot of reasons that your obsessional doubt exists. The narrative that OCD tells you, your obsessional story, is full of details, experiences, facts, and "evidence" to make the obsessional doubt feel so scary and real. This leads to inferential confusion in which you may start mistaking this obsessional story, built in the imagination, for reality. Combining these reasons can help you discover your obsessional story and how you are getting absorbed into it.

As an example, here is an obsessional story based on the obsessional doubt, *What if I get dirty standing over a trash can?*

> *I stand above the trash can. It is possible I am now contaminated. The trash can is dirty. I have touched the trash can before and wound up with something gross on my hands, which proves it is dirty. Though I may not be able to see germs in the air above my trash can, germs exist, they can be invisible, and airborne. I have gotten sick before from airborne germs and viruses, so it could happen again but from a trash can this time. I have been taught to wash my hands if I am dirty and to be cautious around dirty*

items. Especially after the pandemic, we are supposed to be washing our hands, avoiding contaminated items, and not breathing in airborne germs. I once heard a story about someone that got sick after being around piles of garbage, so it is possible that the air above a trash can is dirty and is going to contaminate me. Now I need to wash my hands.

That's quite the convincing story, right?! Even if this obsessional doubt does not bother you, you could see why someone would get stuck on this idea. The obsessional story feels so credible and full of detail, you could get pulled into it, acting as if it is really happening, and engaging in compulsions.

EXERCISE: Now it is your turn to write out your obsessional story. As a template: Start with your trigger; the thing that starts your obsessional sequence. Then combine the reasons into a narrative format, as if you are telling a story. Make it as detailed as possible, in the present tense, and from a first-person perspective.

_____

_____

_____

_____

_____

_____

_____

Notice your reaction when you read back your story. Does your anxiety increase? Does your heart begin racing? Do you feel the urge to engage in a reassurance compulsion? Observe this feeling. This is you getting absorbed into the OCD bubble—mistaking the imaginative story for reality. Compulsions only occur in the OCD bubble. When you are not in the OCD bubble, you do not feel the need to engage in compulsions. Continue along to learn steps to get out of the OCD bubble so the reassurance compulsions stop.

Imagination vs. Perception

While your obsessional story may be filled with a lot of seemingly reliable evidence, experiences, and facts, the story itself is built in the imagination. There is no direct evidence in the here and now that makes it credible. If there were, then it wouldn't be an obsessional doubt; it would be a reasonable doubt.

One step to keep from getting absorbed into the OCD bubble is to use our perception, which is our ability to create awareness through our senses—touch, sight, smell, sound, and taste. To demonstrate this, answer the following question.

How do you know that you're reading the workbook right now?

_____

_____

_____

_____

You probably used a lot of sensory information, such as:

• I can see the book in front of me.

• I feel the weight of the book in my hands.

• I see the words on the page.

• I can hear the book as I flip pages.

Let's try another example. Think back to the last piece of food you ate. How do you know you ate it?

_____

_____

_____

_____

Again, you probably used your perception, meaning information from your senses, to verify this:

• I saw the food.

• I felt the food between my fingers (or the fork in my hand).

• I smelled the food.

• I tasted the food when I bit into it.

• I heard the crunch of the food.

• I felt the food between my teeth.

• I felt the food going down my throat as I swallowed it.

These are examples of how we use perception all day, every day, to determine what we know to be true. Now compare perception to your imagination. Imagination includes all the ideas subjectively generated in our mind. Your obsessional story is built 100 percent in the imagination, has no direct evidence in the here and now, and therefore is irrelevant to this present moment.

OCD can easily create an obsessional story, built in the imagination, about anything. Let's take the example above of "How do you know that you're reading the workbook right now?" An obsessional story might sound like:

I see this workbook and wonder if I'm actually reading it right now. I could be dreaming. I have dreamt a million times. Sometimes my dreams feel so real that I don't know I am dreaming until I wake up. Maybe that is happening to me right now. I have heard of other people that dream but don't know it's a dream. Maybe I just haven't woken up yet. It's possible! Maybe I should pinch myself just to be sure.

You may not get frightened by this obsessional story because it is not an obsession of yours. But you could imagine someone with OCD, especially someone with existential obsessions, having this doubt. That story might sound so convincing, they engage in reassurance compulsions. They might ask their loved ones if they are really reading the workbook or if they are dreaming. They might search on the internet how to know if you are really awake or dreaming. They might pinch themselves to see if they can feel it. They might even provide self-reassurance, saying, *I know I'm awake, I know I'm awake.*

EXERCISE: To continue to understand this difference between perception and imagination, take the obsession *What if a meteor is about to hit me?*

Using your senses or perception, describe what you know to be true at this moment. What can you see or hear that tells you whether you are about to get hit by a meteor?

_____

_____

_____

_____

_____

You may have described how you do not see a meteor coming toward Earth. You may have said that you do not hear any rumbling. You may have described how you did not see anything on the news about a meteor. Or how you do not feel the ground shaking.

Now, create an imaginative, convincing obsessional story about how a meteor is about to hit you.

_____

_____

_____

_____

_____

Here is an example of an obsessional story, built in the imagination, that has no relevance to the present moment. Your story might sound similar or might include completely different information than mine. There is no wrong answer; multiple imaginative stories can exist at the same time.

> *I look out the window and think that a meteor is about to hit me. It is possible. Thousands of meteors hit Earth every year. Some meteors are so big that they could crush my house, with me in it. I have seen stories on the news about meteors hitting Earth and the damage they can cause. It is important to take caution from dangerous things so that I do not get hurt or die. It could happen any minute. I should probably take cover just in case.*

EXERCISE: It is time to apply this idea of imagination versus perception to your obsessional doubt and story. This is one technique to practice when trying to pull yourself out of the OCD bubble, so that you do not engage in those last reassurance compulsions. Using your obsessional story you wrote about your OCD, answer the following questions.

Is there any direct evidence, using your perception, that tells you this obsessional story is actually occurring right now? Anything you can see, feel, hear, smell, or taste, that confirms your obsessional doubt?

_____

_____

_____

_____

What information would you need from the here and now that would tell you this story is actually occurring? What would you need to see, feel, hear, smell, or taste to know that this is not an obsessional doubt? What information would you need to perceive to know it is really happening?

Begin to trust your senses and what you know to be true. If you can recognize that your obsessional story is built in the imagination, using your senses, you will improve your ability to step outside the bubble and see it for what it is: a really creative, convincing, scary story, and that is all. It has no relevance to the present moment. As you gain confidence that this obsessional story is not reality, you will not feel the need to engage in reassurance compulsions. If you still believe the reassurance compulsions are necessary, it is because you are still in the bubble.

The Bridge

Imagine yourself standing in the middle of a bridge. Close your eyes for a moment if it helps you visualize the bridge. On one end of the bridge is a world of imagination. This includes the OCD bubble, where your OCD lives. This imaginative world tries to play tricks on you to make you feel like it is really happening. But in the end, it is just a creative and convincing story that OCD is using to pull you down the bridge into this world of imagination. Notice any thoughts and parts of your obsessional story that try to pull you in.

As you stand in the middle of the bridge, you can also see that at the other end is the here and now. This world includes the present moment. This world includes information you perceive through your five senses. It includes everything that is happening right now in front of you that you know to be true.

Now pause in the middle of this bridge as you observe these two worlds. Hold still as you notice that you are in between these two worlds. Notice that you have a choice in which direction of the bridge you walk toward. The world of imagination is trying to draw you in, with all of its "evidence" and reasons for why you need to engage in reassurance compulsions. There might even be a specific thought that draws you in more. Recognize any thoughts that try to get you to cross over.

As you feel this lure to walk toward the OCD bubble and the urge to engage in a reassurance compulsion, pause. Stand still on the bridge and feel the void. The void is a space where you notice what it feels like to *not* engage in your reassurance compulsions. The void might feel uncomfortable, but pause and sit with that anyway.

Effortlessly use your perception to take in information about what is happening in the present moment. What do you see, hear, smell, taste, or feel? What do you know to be true? Casually observe this, without putting too much effort into this observation. This is all the information you need. Trying to gather more information through your reassurance compulsions would mean not only that you were already in the bubble, but also that you would be pulled further and further into the imagination and away from reality.

At this time, you can make a choice about which direction you want to walk toward by trusting your senses and what you know to be true. Which world do you want to live in? Which world do you want to act on? Your reassurance compulsions do not happen in the world of the here and now. When you are living in the present moment, you do not feel the need to engage in these rituals.

EXERCISE: As you paused in the middle of the bridge, how did it feel to not walk into the OCD bubble? Was it uncomfortable? Were you relieved? Was it difficult?

_____

_____

_____

What thoughts were coming up that tried to pull you into the bubble? Notice how these thoughts are built in the imagination.

_____

_____

_____

_____

What information from your senses did you gather in the present moment? Notice that this is all the information you need. Engaging in reassurance compulsions only pulls you further into the bubble and into the imagination.

_____

_____

_____

_____

If you chose to walk down the bridge to the here and now, how did it feel? Was it uncomfortable not to engage in reassurance compulsions? Was it a relief to trust your senses and act on information that you knew to be true?

_____

_____

_____

Continue practicing these steps, as you are in the middle of the bridge between these two worlds. You are learning to trust yourself again. You are learning to trust your senses again. You are learning to trust what you know to be true. You can still notice and acknowledge the imaginative world where your OCD lives, while choosing to walk in the other direction to the here and now.

Alternative Story

One last technique to assist you in trusting your senses and not getting absorbed into the OCD bubble is to create your alternative story. Just like your obsessional story, the alternative story is one possible story. The alternative story is not used to replace the obsessional story or to make it go away; that would be compulsive. The alternative story is not used to challenge the obsessional story or say it is "wrong." Instead, you are learning that multiple stories can exist at the same time, yet you can choose the story that feels the most convincing and has the most evidence from the here and now.

To better understand how multiple stories can exist at the same time, imagine that you ask a waiter for water, and he brings you some. For many of us, one story you may tell yourself is:

> _I asked for a glass of water. The waiter sets a glass of water in front of me. It looks like water. It is clear. It has no smell. It tastes like water. It must be water._

That is one story that exists. However, you could create many stories about this glass of water. Here is a story built in the imagination:

> _I asked for a glass of water. The waiter sets a glass of water in front of me. What if he poisoned it? Poison could be clear so it would still look like water. I have heard of people being poisoned before. Maybe the waiter or someone in the kitchen is trying to harm me. It is possible._

Now, that story might seem outrageous to you, because you know it is built in the imagination and there is no information in the here and now to make it credible. However, you can imagine how someone with contamination OCD might believe this story anyway. Let's explore another possible story:

I asked for a glass of water. The waiter sets a glass of water in front of me. What if I just lost control of my body and threw the glass of water on him? I have heard stories where people lost control and did something impulsive. One time I got so mad, I threw a pillow at my significant other. It could happen!

That story may sound ridiculous as well, but for someone that fears losing control, this could be a possible obsessional story of theirs.

One last possible story:

I asked for a glass of water. The waiter sets a glass of water in front of me. It looks like a glass of water but maybe I am hallucinating. I could be losing my mind and seeing things that are not really there. It is possible that I am not seeing things correctly.

For someone with obsessions surrounding their mental health, whether that's a fear of schizophrenia or hallucinating, this is a common obsessional story.

The purpose of these stories is to show you that multiple stories can exist in any situation. More stories could be created about that glass of water, such as how that glass of water has been cursed (scrupulous). Or how that glass of water will give you a brain tumor (physical health). Or how that glass of water is actually a hologram (existential). But the ability to create multiple stories does not mean these stories are actually happening in the here and now.

So, now you are going to construct your alternative story. The alternative story is going to consist of as much here-and-now evidence as possible. Continue to develop this alternative story over time, adding more and more details, until it is more convincing than the obsessional story. Creating a convincing alternative story will help you choose to pull out of the bubble and act on reality instead.

EXERCISE: Begin to create your alternative story. Once again, begin with your trigger. Then begin filling in the story with as much information from your senses as possible. For example, the first story about the water included how you could see the water, how there was no smell to the water, and how it tasted like water. What information from your senses can you include in your alternative story?

_____

_____

_____

_____

_____

Continue to elaborate on your story. Fill it full of rich details. Write it in a story-telling manner, with a beginning, middle, and end. And most importantly, write it as if it is happening to you. Be sure to create an ending to your story. The ending is the opposite of you doing a compulsion; it is you choosing to act on your senses and reality as if things are okay.

_____

_____

_____

_____

_____

As a reminder, your alternative story is not used to replace the obsessional story. You also do not want to read or tell it compulsively to "convince" yourself that your obsessional story is a lie. Doing this could itself become compulsive. Instead, notice when you are about to engage in a reassurance compulsion, when you are almost in the bubble, and casually read through your alternative story. This step can assist you with walking away from the bubble, back into the here and now.

Combine these techniques from I-CBT to further eliminate your reassurance compulsions and fully live in the here and now.

Key Takeaways

✓ The OCD bubble is a land of imagination where your OCD lives. If you are engaging in reassurance compulsions, then you are already in the bubble.

✓ Identify the reasons behind your obsessional doubt and the obsessional story your OCD is telling you. This helps you understand how you are getting absorbed into the bubble in the first place.

✓ As you recognize how your story is built in the imagination, therefore irrelevant to the here and now, you will be able to step out of the bubble. You will be able to act on the here and now and what you know to be true.

✓ Imagine yourself standing in the middle of a bridge, between these two worlds: imagination and the here and now. Observe and acknowledge both. Choose which direction you want to walk toward.

✓ Utilize alternative stories as needed, to create another convincing story that actually has here-and-now evidence.

Notes

Congratulations on completing part 2 of this workbook! You now have several techniques to eliminate your reassurance compulsions. You can use these techniques together, or if you find certain strategies that you connect with better than others, use those. Jot down any additional notes here about your obsessional story, information your senses tell you, or alternative stories.

_____

_____

_____

_____

_____

_____

_____

_____

_____

PART 3

When Your Reassurance Involves Others

CHAPTER 10

Reassurance and Your Loved Ones

At this point in your journey, you have learned many new techniques to resist your reassurance compulsions. Hopefully, you are beginning to experience some relief as you refocus your life on the things and people you love.

The people you love may include your family, significant other, or friends. Loved ones are often the main source of our reassurance seeking compulsions, so this chapter provides additional strategies to reduce compulsions that involve them. Your loved ones are often the target of your reassurance compulsions because:

- They may be more available in your day-to-day life, which makes it easier to seek reassurance.

- You feel most comfortable around them to be your true self, OCD and all.

- Your loved ones naturally want to make you feel better, and sometimes that is by participating in your compulsions.

The typical forms of reassurance compulsions we involve our loved ones in are 1) asking them questions, and 2) making statements or confessions. Here is an example of what this can look like in a family system:

Preston is a twelve-year-old boy who has struggled with OCD for a couple years. His primary obsession is that something bad is going to happen, especially regarding his home and family. This results in a lot of checking, reassurance questions, and routines that involve his parents. Preston will ask his parents multiple times in a day, "Is everything okay?" and his parents have to respond in a positive manner, otherwise he becomes extremely distressed. Preston also engages in a repetitive routine in which he says, "I love you, Mom. I love you, Dad. I am thankful for you." His parents respond, "We love you Preston. We are thankful for you." If his parents do not respond in this manner, Preston has to begin his compulsive statement again. "I love you, Mom. I love you, Dad. I am thankful for you." He explains that sometimes, even when they do say it correctly, it doesn't "feel right" so he starts over and repeats until it does feel right. In addition, Preston checks the home, all doors, and all appliances to make sure nothing bad happens. Some evenings, he will ask his parents to check after he does just in case he missed something important.

EXERCISE: How were Preston's parents involved in his compulsions?

_____

_____

_____

_____

Which loved ones do you involve the most in your reassurance compulsions?

_____

_____

What do those reassurance compulsions look like?

_____

_____

_____

_____

_____

_____

Impact on Loved Ones

Sean experiences moral obsessions, in which he constantly wonders if he made a wrong or immoral choice. He reports his main compulsion is in the form of reassurance, in which he asks his friends and significant other if the choices he made are okay or if he is a bad person. His obsessional doubts about morality include tipping enough at a restaurant, going a mile over the speed limit while driving, or taking change he finds on the sidewalk (as it might be considered stealing).

In addition to asking his friends and significant other if he made a bad decision following these sorts of events, he will continue asking questions like "But how do you know?" and "Are you sure?" This has led to much frustration on their part. Some of his friends are even threatening to stop speaking to Sean until he quits. Sean fears losing his loved ones but is unsure how to quit asking these questions, as the urge is so strong.

This chapter is dedicated to when reassurance compulsions involve your loved ones, because the impact can be detrimental to relationships. Chapter 5 shared examples of the effect reassurance compulsions can have on your loved ones, and chapter 10 emphasizes why strategies are needed in these situations and how to talk to your loved ones about it.

Parents and caregivers often report a combination of sadness, frustration, anxiety, and hopelessness, among other feelings. It is common for people to go to family members, like their parents, to provide the relief they are looking for. This can lead to strains in the parent-child relationship, fighting, or an accommodating relationship in which a loved one becomes part of your compulsion. Parents and caregivers often report hopelessness and are uncertain how to respond, as they do not want to make things worse but are unsure of what to do.

If you have a significant other, you may have given them reassurance of some kind. Mutual support and empathy are a common part of a loving relationship, and giving reassurance can sometimes be warranted. But as we know, not all forms of reassurance are healthy, and that includes when it becomes a compulsion for your OCD. Telling the difference between the two can be confusing for yourself and your significant other, because the two of you may not know when it is OCD and when it is okay to respond. Or if you are aware of the difference, the two of you may not know what other options there are. Feeling stuck in an unhealthy pattern can lead to tension, conflict, irritation with each other, and even difficulty with intimacy.

But your loved ones can also include your friends, colleagues, extended family, or your children—the people that matter most to you in the world. You may fear you are driving them off with your constant questions or statements, which will just contribute to additional feelings like sadness and shame. You may notice loved ones avoiding certain interactions with you in fear of triggering your OCD or hearing the dreaded reassurance questions again. The toll your OCD and reassurance compulsions have on your loved ones can motivate you to continue your journey and implement the upcoming strategies.

Based on the loved ones you identified earlier, have you noticed your reassurance compulsions impacting your relationships in any way? What is happening or what do you fear might happen?

_____

_____

_____

_____

_____

_____

Family Accommodations

Family accommodation is a term often associated with anxiety disorders and OCD. Family accommodation refers to when your loved ones become part of your ritual or avoidance. In other words, they provide accommodations, or adjustments, for your OCD. The idea of family accommodation can be easily confused with helpful accommodations made for individuals needing assistance in specific situations. For example, an individual who is diagnosed with attention deficit/hyperactivity disorder or a learning disability and needs testing accommodations at school, like extra time on a test or testing in a quiet room. Or an individual who needs environmental accommodations, like ramps and wider doorways, due to being in a wheelchair.

In the OCD world, family accommodations are an important part of your treatment to identify; you can be taking all the right steps, but if accommodations are still done for you, you will only make so much progress. Accommodations are just another form of a compulsion.

So, what do family accommodations with OCD look like? Family members may:

- Provide reassurance for you

- Provide items necessary to do a compulsion, like hand sanitizer or Wi-Fi

- Take on household tasks that you may not be able to do because of OCD, like taking out the trash or cleaning the bathrooms

- Complete personal tasks for you for which your OCD impairs your ability to do yourself, like bathing or getting dressed

- Complete the compulsion for you, like checking a door knob or washing food

- Help you avoid things or situations that trigger your anxiety

- Avoid talking about topics that may be triggering

- Avoid doing things that may lead to an obsession or compulsion

- Provide you with more time to engage in compulsions

- Make decisions for you because your OCD makes it difficult to do

- Give up leisure activities or change their schedule to accommodate your OCD

Have you and your loved ones participated in any of these family accommodations? Are there any additional accommodations you recognize?

_____

_____

_____

_____

Recommendations

Seeking and receiving reassurance from loved ones is the most common family accommodation. It is natural to ask your loved ones to feel better and it is natural for them to want to make you feel better. However, family accommodations have similar long-term impacts to engaging in compulsions yourself. These accommodations may provide short-term relief, but in the long term, they reinforce and worsen anxiety. Reassurance breeds more reassurance to the point that you find it necessary to ask your loved ones these questions. So, continue reading for specific recommendations to reduce family accommodation.

Supportive vs. Reassuring Responses

In this section, you will be taught the difference between a reassuring response and a supportive response. You will be able to identify what responses to OCD feel nurturing, not shaming or harmful. As you know, reassuring responses are designed to relieve your doubt…for a moment. Reassuring responses might sound like:

- It's fine.

- You're okay.

- Don't worry about it.

- Nothing bad is going to happen.

- That would never happen.

- You're safe.

- That's illogical; that's not true.

- That's silly, it won't happen.

As you are already aware, these responses may feel relieving for a moment, but anxiety will soon return and possibly even worsen. Instead, a supportive statement conveys a message that this moment of anxiety or discomfort may be difficult, but you can manage it! It encourages you to continue working hard toward your journey and that your support system is here for you. Supportive statements include a sentiment of validation and instillation of confidence (Lebowitz 2021), and may sound like:

- I know this is hard, but I believe in you.

- I can tell you are anxious, and I know you can handle this.

- I believe this may be a compulsion, what do you think? What else could we try?

- I know this is difficult for you. I am here for you.

- It sounds like your OCD is causing a lot of distress for you. What would your therapist recommend right now?

- I can tell you really want an answer from me. I bet we can do something else that will be more helpful for you.

- I love you and want to help you when you're anxious. What if we pull out your workbook to see what skills would be useful right now?

The number of options for supportive statements are endless—those are just a few of my favorites. Maybe you connect well with one of those statements or maybe you have another statement in mind. The goal is to identify one (or two) that feel supportive, understanding, and validating. You want to choose one that will not feel harsh or shaming, but rather comforting and encouraging.

Write down a few supportive statements that are a good fit for you. You may choose one of the above or create one of your own.

_____

_____

_____

_____

_____

_____

Reassurance Contracting

Now that you have identified a supportive statement or two, it is time to inform your support system that you need their help, if you are comfortable doing so. As a reminder, you are never required to tell anyone about your OCD. However, if you often involve loved ones in your compulsions, you may find it helpful to receive their support.

The process we will review next is reassurance contracting, in which you make an agreement with your support system on how you would like them to respond to your reassurance compulsions. This contract also educates your support system on what your reassurance compulsions look and sound like, why you are trying to decrease these compulsions, how you will reach your overall goal of eliminating them, and how they can respond when you slip up.

You may prefer to do reassurance contracting with the help of a professional; however, you can also do it on your own. The following steps outline the process for reassurance contracting.

Step 1. Gather your loved ones whom you often involve in family accommodation, meaning they participate in your compulsions, provide you reassurance, or allow for avoidance.

Step 2. Share important information with your loved ones. What you say depends on how comfortable you are and how much you want to share. This information might include what your OCD diagnosis looks like, or how your obsessions and compulsions work. Provide examples of what your reassurance compulsions look like, especially any that involve your loved ones, like asking them repetitive questions.

Step 3. Provide psychoeducation on OCD, the OCD cycle, and why you are choosing to eliminate reassurance compulsions. Share the impact that these compulsions have on your life and relationships. Explain that while you have worked very hard to resist asking reassurance questions and other forms of compulsions, they can be difficult to resist, and this is where you need support.

Step 4. Share the supportive statements you created earlier. Explain why these kinds of statements are more beneficial to your OCD in the long run than reassuring statements. Inquire if your loved ones would be willing to respond with these supportive statements going forward.

Write a sample script below of how you can approach reassurance contracting with your loved one:

_____

_____

_____

_____

_____

_____

_____

_____

I hope that this reassurance-contracting process provides you the additional support you need while also reducing the reassurances your OCD is seeking out. Continue to make adjustments, especially with your supportive statements, if you notice any adverse reaction to them. While it is expected you will be anxious and uncomfortable at first when you do not receive the reassurance your OCD wants, if you are noticing other reactions to the support, it might not be the best response for you. Make modifications when needed, continue to practice your strategies to resist compulsions, and enjoy the progress.

Non-Engagement Responses

In addition to the supportive statements above, you can incorporate non-engagement responses with your support system and use them by yourself. Non-engagement responses are a technique to answer your reassurance questions without giving them the power and answers your OCD is looking for (Levine 2020). In a sense, these non-engagement responses can also be a form of exposure, depending on the level of anxiety they provoke. Choose from several different types of non-engagement responses, which range in ease.

A common non-engagement response is responding with the acknowledgment of *anxiety*. This is similar to the concept of defusion, an ACT technique. Defusion can help you create space between you and your thoughts, feelings, and sensations. By noticing and labeling the anxiety that is present instead of seeking reassurance for your obsessions, you distance yourself from the thought and give it less power. Non-engagement responses might sound like:

- *That makes me anxious.*

- *I notice I am uncomfortable.*

- *That brings up some anxiety.*

- *That thought is nerve-wracking.*

- *I notice anxiety present.*

Choose whatever wording feels best for you, and you can use it with yourself when you have the urge to ask others reassurance questions. You can also provide these statements to your loved ones. They can respond similarly with "That sounds nerve-wracking" or "I can tell that makes you anxious."

You may choose to respond with *uncertainty*. This non-engagement response conveys a message that you do not know the answer to your question or you can never be certain of the answer. This is a simple response that your loved ones may feel more comfortable using. These uncertain non-engagement responses can sound like:

- Who knows?

- I don't know.

- I'm uncertain about that.

- We'll see.

- I can't answer that.

- *shrug*

Next, and a personal favorite, is responding with *possibility*. This non-engagement response expresses that there is always a possibility of anything happening, including your obsession. It is important to note that this non-engagement response might be the most anxiety provoking, because it does not negate the fact that anything is possible. Even your obsessional doubt. It can even be an exposure for the positive possibility of your obsession. However, some individuals might consider it the most light-hearted and humorous of the strategies. Responding with possibility could range from:

- Maybe.

- Possibly.

- That is possible.

- I guess that could totally happen.

- Anything could happen.

- I've seen bizarre things happen before.

- There's always a chance.

- Totally.

Imagine if you went to your loved one asking, "Am I going to die?" and their response was "Totally!" You might have an unpleasant reaction at first to their response, as it was too big of an exposure too fast, without your consent. It is best to use this specific non-engagement response further along in your journey, when you are ready to allow for more possibility and uncertainty in the world. It is also essential that your loved ones do not utilize uncertainty responses without your consent. Please have a discussion with your loved ones first about when you are ready to add *possibility* into your responses. Yet there is a reason these are my personal favorite…they are exactly the opposite of what your OCD wants to hear! Allowing yourself to recognize that anything is possible, but that it is not necessarily happening in the present moment, is essential in breaking the OCD cycle.

Last, your loved ones can respond by expressing the *difficulty* they would have—how much it would pain them—if your obsessional doubt actually happened. There can be a sense of humor in these responses as well, which may appeal to you. Responding with *difficulty* may sound like:

- That would totally suck.

- Well, that would be awful.

- Oooh, I don't like that.

- I don't like the idea of that.

- That's just a terrible idea.

- Yep, that would be horrible. Oh well.

If these responses are a good fit for you, please share them with your loved ones. Imagine if you asked, "Do you think I have cancer?" and their response was, "Well, that would be awful." Or if you repeatedly asked, "Is someone going to break into our house?" and they responded with, "Yep, that would be horrible. Oh well." Your OCD wouldn't know what to do with that response at first, but eventually you would recognize that you can tolerate not receiving the reassurance you want, and you might even find a little humor in it.

So, take your pick. Do you like the sound of any of these non-engagement responses? Which would you like your loved ones to use? Maybe you even thought of a few of your own. Jot them down here and be sure to share them with your loved ones.

_____

_____

_____

_____

_____

_____

Reassurance Notebooks

The last intervention I recommend to reduce reassurance is one we often see used with children. However, it is also appropriate for adults and it may be a helpful step in reducing your reassurance questions.

Now, in an ideal world, you would eliminate all reassurance compulsions. But sometimes that is such a difficult endeavor that you need a "stepping stone," or a small move in the direction of reducing the compulsion, with the intention of eventually eliminating it. This is where a reassurance notebook could come in handy.

Dedicate a notebook to be your reassurance notebook; for children, let them have fun and decorate the notebook. Instead of asking your loved ones the reassurance questions you want, write them in the reassurance notebook. The loved one, whether that be a parent, a significant other, or another person in your support system, will review the questions in the notebook. Your loved one may start off with reviewing them once a day, but then as you progress, decrease the frequency to every other day, then once a week, then every other week, then once a month, until eventually the loved one no longer needs to review the book. As time passes and your loved one is no longer reviewing the reassurance notebook, the urge to even write in it will decrease too.

Your loved one can do a few different things when reviewing the reassurance notebook, depending on where you are at in your journey. They may start off with answering the questions once. Any duplicate questions in the future will not be answered, rather responded to with a supportive statement like "I believe you know this answer. I have confidence in you that you can handle this anxiety!"

As you become more and more comfortable not getting your repetitive reassurance questions answered, your loved one may respond with writing an "uncertain" response or a non-engagement response. This might look like your loved one responding with "Who knows," "Maybe," or "I guess that's a possibility." You can continue to write your reassurance questions in the notebook if you have the urge, but you are aware that you are not going to receive reassurance back.

Now that you are making more and more progress and getting comfortable with the non-engagement responses, your loved one can then move on to simply reviewing the questions, but not providing any written response. This stepping stone allows you to ask your questions but receive no answers. You can continue to write your questions in the notebook if you feel the urge to and know that someone will read them, but you will not receive any response back.

And the final step is…write down your reassurance questions in the reassurance notebook without anyone reviewing it. This last step allows you to continue writing your questions down with the understanding that no one is going to read them anymore.

As discussed, this is a great intervention for children but adults may also find it very helpful in gradually reducing their reassurance compulsions. Try starting your reassurance notebook today. Over time, reflect on how it goes. Was it difficult? Easy? How is the process going for you?

_____

_____

_____

_____

_____

My Story

I noticed a few different types of family accommodation occurring after I got married. My just-right OCD greatly disliked things being out of place. When I lived alone, it was easy to accommodate this myself, as I simply put things where I wanted and compulsively fixed items as I felt the urge.

But living with a spouse meant 1) an increase in fixing compulsions because more and more items were moved out of place, and 2) my encouraging him to fix things for me as well. Through my constant requests (which on the outside looked like nagging but it was a distressing urge to have him fix items), I basically taught him how to become part of my compulsion.

I made him put away clean laundry in the exact way I felt it needed to be folded, placed in drawers, or hung in the closet. I became irritated and had him line items up in the pantry how I felt they should go. I had specific blankets that went in specific places and he learned where they needed to go. I "taught" him what items were not to be moved. The examples were endless, as I thought I was managing the distress of items being out of place. But really, I was only worsening anxiety by having him comply.

The other family accommodation I pulled my spouse into was the constant reassurance questions about cleanliness. It took a lot of time for me to recognize that I was asking him these questions. My contamination obsessions had me constantly questioning if an item is contaminated or safe. And when I had children, this increased, as I constantly worried about the kids' cleanliness and them touching items in the home.

I would question his cleaning abilities and encourage him to clean more: countertops, dishes, toilets, cars, bedding, and more. I would ask him if things were clean, when he last cleaned things, or if it was okay to touch something.

Looking back, I can recognize how I put my compulsions onto him. However, it ultimately caused tension and conflict in our relationship. Over time, he learned how to provide support instead of accommodation, and I utilized many of the techniques from the former chapters to decrease my compulsions, including response prevention strategies, mindfulness, living my values and stepping outside of the OCD bubble.

Key Takeaways

✓ Family accommodation occurs when our loved ones become part of our compulsion or avoidance. Reassurance compulsions often involve your loved ones because they are most readily available, you feel comfortable around them, and they want you to feel better.

✓ This can impact your relationships with loved ones and you may experience increased conflict, tension, or difficulties with them. Some loved ones may avoid interactions with you or be driven away.

✓ Strategies to reduce family accommodation include creating supportive statements, making a reassurance contract, using non-engagement responses, and utilizing a reassurance notebook.

Notes

You have taken many steps toward eliminating reassurance compulsions, and now your loved ones are ready to support you in this journey. As you practice the skills in this chapter, feel free to tweak your supportive statements if needed and inform your support system. Practice your non-engagement responses and identify additional ones that fit you well. Make note of these new ideas and any other helpful information below.

_____

_____

_____

_____

_____

_____

_____

_____

_____

_____

_____

CHAPTER 11

Reassurance and Your Providers

Janine is seeing a therapist, weekly, to manage her OCD. She constantly wonders if she has said something offensive, whether in an email, via text, or in person. This obsession leads to reassurance seeking compulsions involving others—asking if she said anything wrong or asking if they are upset with her.

Throughout treatment, Janine has made a lot of progress decreasing her reassurance seeking from loved ones. However, she did not realize she transferred this reassurance compulsion onto her therapist. Janine began emailing her therapist in the middle of the night, attaching screenshots of text conversations. She would ask in her email, "Do you think this sounds fine?" In the sessions, Janine would review situations from the past week and inquire, "Do you think that was offensive?" On a few occasions, Janine would call and ask for a sooner appointment to discuss if a conversation she had was offensive or not.

At first, Janine's therapist did not realize she had become part of the reassurance compulsions. The therapist wanted to be compassionate and build a trusting relationship with her client, so she often provided this reassurance. With all of the progress made in treatment, Janine continued to struggle with the anxiety surrounding her obsessions, because she unknowingly was still engaging in her reassurance compulsions with her therapist.

This vignette is a common one, in which your providers and other important people in your world can become part of the OCD cycle and engage in reassurance compulsions with you. These compulsions often go missed because you may assume that your reassurance seeking can't be a compulsion if your therapist provides the answer. Or it can't be a problem if your doctor answers your questions. Or it must not be harmful if your religious leader provides reassurance, as religious leaders would never do anything to worsen your mental health.

In some instances, providers get pulled into compulsions because of a lack of knowledge or education on OCD. In other instances, it may be because they feel they are helping or providing support, and want to see your anxiety decrease. As you have learned, though, your anxiety only decreases momentarily. Providing reassurance compulsively is not actually aiding in your recovery and there are more helpful ways to provide support.

Providers

You may seek reassurance from a variety of providers or people you deem as *experts*. The hope is that these providers will be able to give you an answer that resolves the obsession. You may believe that if they tell you "Everything is fine" or "That would never happen," you will finally believe it and no longer struggle with this obsession.

The variety of providers you engage in these reassurance compulsions may include:

- Primary care physicians, nurse practitioners, physician assistants, RNs

- Specialists—pediatricians, OB-GYNs, endocrinologists, neurologists, dermatologists, cardiologists, etc.

- Dentists

- Chiropractors

- Psychiatrists

- Mental health therapists

- Pharmacists

You might also engage people who are not health care providers. While they may not work in the health care field, they may be individuals you see as knowledgeable and trustworthy. They may serve an important role in your life, whether they help you, teach you, or provide you support. They can include:

- Religious leaders

- Spiritual healers

- Holistic providers and naturopaths

- Teachers and professors

- Social media influencers

- Coaches

- Mentors

- Consultants and advisors

Reassurance seeking can target any of these individuals; however, it may show up differently given their role in your life. Let's explore what reassurance compulsions with these individuals look like.

Reassurance Compulsion Examples

Medical providers, such as your primary doctor, are common targets of reassurance seeking with OCD. This is especially the case if you experience health obsessions—however you might seek reassurance for contamination, death, existential, postpartum obsessions, and more. These compulsions can look like:

- Calling your doctor or their nurse excessively to relieve the anxiety from obsessions
  - Asking about symptoms you are experiencing
  - Inquiring about illnesses you are fearful of
  - Constantly checking about medications you are on and side effects
- Messaging your doctor or their nurse excessively through your medical chart
- Scheduling an abundance of appointments
- Requesting unnecessary medical procedures, tests, and blood work
- "Shopping around" for doctors by seeking multiple providers and second opinions

Similar reassurance compulsions may occur with your mental health care providers, such as your therapist or psychiatrist. You may not realize it is a reassurance compulsion, as it is assumed that mental health care providers would never do anything to worsen your mental health. However, they are often doing it unknowingly. And your therapist or psychiatrist may not realize it was a reassurance compulsion if they do not have the specialty training needed to fully understand OCD, its nuances, and what reassurance compulsions look like. Examples include:

- Calling your therapist or psychiatrist excessively with reassurance questions, even if you already know the answer
- Emailing these providers with questions to relieve anxiety surrounding your obsession
- Asking repetitive reassurance questions in session to feel immediate relief
- Confessing obsessions
- Staring for reactions

Meta OCD is a particular subtype that targets therapists, in which you question if you really have OCD. In short, meta OCD includes obsessions about obsessions or doubts about your OCD. This may come in the form of questions like:

- Are you sure I really have OCD?
- What if I don't actually have OCD?
- What if I made it all up?
- What if I'm lying to you?
- Is this thought actually OCD? Maybe the others were but this one is different.

Religious leaders and other spiritual healers are frequently the target for reassurance on religious and scrupulous obsessions (however, you may discuss questions from any subtype with clergy). It is natural for an individual to seek out their religious leader when they have religious or scrupulous obsessions, which sound like *Am I a bad person? Have I sinned?* or *Am I being punished?* And perhaps neither of you realizes when it crosses the line from value to compulsion.

Confessing is another common reassurance compulsion involving religious leaders. For example:

- Telling your religious leader that you had an "inappropriate thought" so they can absolve you of any sin

- Sharing your sexual obsessions and watching their reaction to the confession

- Confessing all of the "bad" things you feel you have done

- Sharing all of your fears about being punished by a higher being or what will happen in the afterlife

Anyone can be a target, though, not just spiritual leaders. You may excessively message a social media influencer that has OCD, sharing your obsessions, hoping they will say "That is normal" or "Don't worry about that." You may constantly ask questions of your teacher or professor, inquiring if you made any mistakes. No one is off limits, and as always, the first step in decreasing reassurance compulsions is increasing your awareness of when they are happening.

EXERCISE: After reviewing the different providers and examples of reassurance compulsions, who have you included in your OCD cycle? Who did you involve in your reassurance compulsions?

_____

_____

_____

_____

What did this look like? What reassurance compulsions did you engage in?

_____

_____

_____

_____

_____

My Story

Once upon a time, I became stuck on the possibility that I had colon cancer. My obsessional story included facts like how my mom had colon cancer and how I had blood in my bowel movements on occasion. My obsessional story included how it was entirely possible that, at the age of 30, I had colon cancer. This story felt so real and so scary, I went down a rabbit hole of reassurance seeking compulsions. Not only did this include reassurance seeking online, by searching WebMD and other health related websites, but it also included reassurance seeking from my doctor.

My reassurance seeking compulsions came in the form of confessing my concerns to my doctor, asking questions, and even asking for a colonoscopy at such a young age. Due to my family history and the blood in my bowel movements (which I knew was minimal and inconsistent), my doctor obliged. It was easy to convince myself that this was not a compulsion, rather I was taking care of my health. I even convinced myself that I was living my values because I was taking care of my health.

But my values with my health do not look like this. My values with my health are to casually, not obsessively, observe symptoms. Notice if pain worsens or eases. Watch for how persistent it is and how long it occurs. Then, based on those values, I might mention something to my doctor.

Fast forward, and to no surprise, I did not have colon cancer. Everything looked fine. This reassurance provided relief like most compulsions do, but it was only temporary and my health obsessions latched onto other concerns. From ovarian cancer to thyroid cancer, I have continued to experience health obsessions for many years.

The difference now is, I do not get pulled into the OCD bubble. I do not give into OCD and engage in reassurance compulsions. I may search ailments and possible diagnoses online one time for educational purposes, but I know doing more than that is a compulsion. I may mention concerns to my doctor if symptoms have been persistent and concerning, but I don't report every sensation I notice.

Psychoeducation

Not everyone understands OCD and reassurance compulsions like you do, unfortunately. While it is not your responsibility to teach the entire world about OCD or become the next OCD advocate, it can be helpful to inform those in your inner circle when you need their support with treatment. Especially if they are caught up in your reassurance compulsions, you will all benefit from teaching them about how your OCD presents, why you seek the reassurance you do, and what the long-term impact is of their engaging in your compulsions.

There are many ways to educate your support network, and you want to find one that is comfortable for you. A common avenue is to provide the individual, whether that be your doctor or your priest, resources on OCD. This may look like sending them the website to the International OCD Foundation, which includes research, articles, and videos on OCD. You may recommend a favorite book written about OCD and OCD treatment—maybe even this workbook! You may pass on your favorite OCD podcast and encourage them to listen to better understand you. You may even share your favorite social media account that provides psychoeducation on OCD. I highly recommend @anxietyocdtreatment on Instagram!

The most helpful way though, is through your own words. Whether in person with this provider or via email, you can advocate for yourself. Share what OCD is, how your obsessions and compulsions appear, and what would be more helpful from your provider. This can be difficult to put into words so an example script is provided below. Feel free to edit it for your specific situation.

Sample Script

I have been diagnosed with OCD, and I feel it is important I share with you some information about my symptoms and treatment. As part of my support system, there are certain aspects of my disorder that may involve you, and it would help me for you to know when this is occurring.

OCD includes unwanted, distressing, persistent, intrusive thoughts called obsessions. My obsessions include:

_____

_____

_____

These obsessions then lead to repetitive rituals I feel like I have to do to find relief or stop the obsessions. These are called compulsions. My compulsions include:

_____

_____

_____

A very common compulsion for myself and many others is reassurance seeking. I attempt to seek reassurance to find immediate relief, and sometimes I seek this reassurance from you. These reassurance seeking questions may sound like:

_____

_____

_____

_____

While providing reassurance can feel supportive and helpful, giving me answers to a reassurance seeking compulsion, as part of my OCD, can actually worsen the disorder. Which is why I have been going through my treatment journey and decreasing these rituals. I am learning to resist these urges, engage in my values, increase my mindfulness, and not get sucked into the scary story my OCD is telling me.

Despite my progress, I am human and sometimes I slip up. This is why I wanted to let you know what my specific reassurance seeking questions sound like, in case it happens again. What I have found to be most helpful is when people provide support and encouragement while not answering the question. This might sound like:

- *I know this is hard, but I believe in you.*

- *I can tell you are anxious. I know you can handle this.*

- *I believe this may be a compulsion. What do you think? What else could we try?*

- *I know this is difficult for you. I am here to support you.*

- *It sounds like your OCD is causing a lot of distress for you. What would your therapist recommend right now?*

- *I can tell you really want an answer from me. I bet we can do something else that will be more helpful for you.*

Please let me know if you have any questions about OCD, my symptoms, or my reassurance seeking compulsions. I know I can make even more progress with the help of my support system.

Final Recommendations

Although you are coming to the end of this workbook, that does not mean you are coming to the end of your journey. There may be a few reassurance compulsions you are still working on. There may be new OCD themes that have popped up along the way (as it so often happens with OCD). Or you simply want to practice the skills from this workbook to maintain your progress.

No matter where you are in your journey and the progress you have made, you can always reflect back on this workbook and the techniques provided. You have practiced a variety of skills to reduce your reassurance compulsions including:

- **Awareness Training:** answer the "who, what, where, when, triggers and emotions" of your compulsions; utilize simple tracking systems, monitoring forms, and reminders; utilize your supports to bring compulsions to your attention; and use code words and signals

- **Response Prevention Strategies:** create a written plan; delay or undo compulsions using opposite action, stimulus control, picking battles, labeling and abandoning; utilize your supports; practice mindfulness

- **Mindfulness:** engage in mindful activities, mindful eating, body scans, and mindful thoughts

- **Values:** identify values and name valued behaviors

- **Pulling yourself out of the OCD bubble:** acknowledge imagination versus perception, imagine the bridge metaphor, and utilize an alternative story

- **Support from loved ones:** recommend supportive statements, non-engagement responses, reassurance contracting, and reassurance notebooks

- **Support from providers:** provide psychoeducation, resources, and scripts

As you continue forward, you may have a favorite technique you utilize. Or you may find a combination of strategies that work well for you. It is even possible that you'll connect well with some skills now, but later connect with others and decide to transition. Keep this workbook so you may review skills as needed to maintain the progress you have made, and continue to progress even further.

Key Takeaways

✓ Reassurance compulsions can target anyone, including people we deem *experts*, like your doctor, psychiatrist, therapist, religious leader, or a coach.

✓ Compulsions may vary depending on the provider. These reassurance compulsions can include excessive questions and emails, scheduling too many appointments, requesting additional testing or lab work, or confessions.

✓ While you are not required to inform anyone of your OCD or teach them about OCD, you may find it helpful in some cases to provide this education. You can give them resources and have conversations.

✓ Decrease your reassurance compulsions with these individuals like you would with others. Utilize your response prevention strategies, techniques to get outside of the OCD bubble, values work, and mindfulness techniques.

Notes

How are you feeling about your progress? As you end your journey through this book, you are probably having mixed emotions. You may be experiencing pride in the work you have completed or fear that it will be difficult to continue. You may even be experiencing some reassurance compulsions still, which is to be expected. Provide yourself some grace and compassion, because treatment does not happen overnight (or in a week or a month!). Continue with the steps throughout this workbook and go back and review as necessary. Jot down any final notes, words of encouragement, or areas you are hoping to address next, below.

_____

_____

_____

_____

_____

_____

_____

_____

_____

_____

_____

References

American Psychiatric Association (APA). 2007. "Practice Guideline for the Treatment of Patients with Obsessive-Compulsive Disorder." Arlington, VA: APA. http://psychiatryonline.org/pb/assets/raw/site wide/practice_guidelines/guidelines/ocd.pdf.

———. 2022. *The Diagnostic and Statistical Manual of Mental Disorders*, 5th ed., text revision. Washington, DC: APA.

Goodman, W. K., L. H. Price, S. A. Rasmussen, C. Mazure, R. L. Fleischmann, C. L. Hill, G. R. Heninger, and D. S. Charney. 1989. "The Yale-Brown Obsessive Compulsive Scale: I. Development, Use, and Reliability." *Archives of General Psychiatry* 46(11): 1006–1011.

Harris, R. 2006. "Embracing Your Demons: An Overview of Acceptance and Commitment Therapy." *Psychotherapy in Australia* 12(4): 1–8.

Hayes, S. C., K. D. Strosahl, and K. G. Wilson. 2003. *Acceptance and Commitment Therapy: An Experiential Approach to Behavior Change*. New York: Guilford Press.

Lebowitz, E. R. 2021. *Breaking Free of Child Anxiety and OCD: A Scientifically Proven Program for Parents*. New York: Oxford University Press.

Levine, L. 2020. "How Do I Stop Thinking About This? What to Do When You're Stuck Playing Mental Ping Pong." *International OCD Foundation OCD Newsletter* 34(2): 10–12.

Linehan, M. M. 2014. *DBT Skills Training Manual*, 2nd ed. New York: Guilford Press.

Miller, W. R., and S. Rollnick. 2012. *Motivational Interviewing: Helping People Change*, 3rd ed. New York: Guilford Press.

O'Connor, K., and R. Aardema. 2012. *Clinician's Handbook for Obsessive Compulsive Disorder: Inference-Based Therapy*. Chichester, UK: Wiley-Blackwell.

Steketee, G. 1999. *Overcoming Obsessive-Compulsive Disorder: A Behavioral and Cognitive Protocol for the Treatment of OCD*. Oakland, CA: New Harbinger Publications.

Amanda Petrik-Gardner, LCPC, is an obsessive-compulsive disorder (OCD) and body-focused repetitive behavior (BFRB) specialist, licensed in multiple states. She is a member of the International OCD Foundation, TLC Foundation for BFRBs, and the Anxiety and Depression Association of America. Amanda is on the board for OCD Kansas, a state affiliate of the International OCD Foundation, and is author of *An OCD Exposure Coloring Book*. She is from Topeka, KS.

Foreword writer **Nathan Peterson, LCSW,** has extensive expertise in the treatment of OCD, anxiety, tics, Tourette's syndrome, and various body-focused repetitive behaviors (BFRBs). He maintains a private practice in Allen, TX.

Real change *is* possible

For more than forty-five years, New Harbinger has
published proven-effective self-help books and pioneering
workbooks to help readers of all ages and backgrounds
improve mental health and well-being, and achieve lasting
personal growth. In addition, our spirituality books
offer profound guidance for deepening awareness and
cultivating healing, self-discovery, and fulfillment.

Founded by psychologist Matthew McKay and Patrick
Fanning, New Harbinger is proud to be an independent,
employee-owned company. Our books reflect our
core values of integrity, innovation, commitment,
sustainability, compassion, and trust. Written by leaders
in the field and recommended by therapists worldwide,
New Harbinger books are practical, accessible, and
provide real tools for real change.

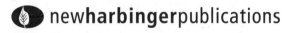 new**harbinger**publications

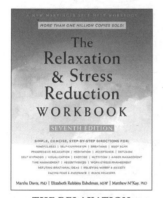

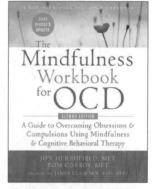

Did you know there are **free tools** you can download for this book?

Free tools are things like **worksheets, guided meditation exercises**, and **more** that will help you get the most out of your book.

You can download free tools for this book— whether you bought or borrowed it, in any format, from any source—from the New Harbinger website. All you need is a NewHarbinger.com account. Just use the URL provided in this book to view the free tools that are available for it. Then, click on the "download" button for the free tool you want, and follow the prompts that appear to log in to your NewHarbinger.com account and download the material.

You can also save the free tools for this book to your **Free Tools Library** so you can access them again anytime, just by logging in to your account! Just look for this button on the book's free tools page.

+ Save this to my free tools library

If you need help accessing or downloading free tools, visit **newharbinger.com/faq** or contact us at **customerservice@newharbinger.com**.